x

sweet

gluten-free desserts
made using healthy &
wholesome ingredients

lina jabbari

I dedicate this book to Grandma, who
manages to sweeten up every occasion

contents

introduction

Sweet foods have always been a big part of my life. I'd never go a day without cakes, cookies, brownies or pastries.

My journey of baking started at age six when I learned how to make eyeball cupcakes at school for Halloween - I became obsessed and I'll never forget the anticipation I felt coming home from school to make them.

I have been lucky enough to grow up under the same roof as Grandma. She's the type of person who finds any excuse to cook or bake for people, whether it was for birthdays, friends coming over, weddings, a weekend or cultural celebrations like Norouz, the Persian New Year. Baking was her way of expressing love to those around her and her food has filled our community with warm memories and pure joy.

As I got older, the comforting associations from childhood cakes, turned into a coping mechanism during times of stress. I comfort ate my way with all things sweet and I started to notice that this had negative implications on my wellbeing. I decided to transition to a more health-conscious lifestyle, which initially meant denying all the sweet things I previously enjoyed. This led me down the not-so-healthy path of restrictive dieting and binge cycles. It was miserable.

Once I realised how my 'healthy lifestyle' was more aligned with the toxic diet culture belief system, I knew I needed to change things up and find balance. Slowly but surely, I did.

I learned how to eat sustainably without feeling deprived by eating more whole foods. Eventually, eating became more intuitive and without intending to, the intense sugar cravings ended.

I wanted to apply the same approach of the way I ate, to the way I baked. By looking into more nutrient-dense ingredients and experimenting a ton with different types of flours, fats and sugars, I was able to replicate the classic recipes I love. With *a lot* of trial and error, I learned it's possible to bake all kinds of desserts without using conventional ingredients.

I found balance in enjoying sweet treats while using wholesome ingredients; not because I needed that sugar hit, but because I wanted to. And yes, they taste freaking delicious! I still have a sweet tooth, but my tastebuds have adjusted to a lower level of sweetness. Baking for my family has shown me that it's necessary to find a happy balance in the level of sweetness of my desserts, to be able to accommodate everyone. Much like salt, sweetness is subjective. It depends on what you're accustomed to; so if you and the people you bake for usually eat 'regular' cakes and cookies, you might find that some of these recipes are slightly less sweet, so you can adjust accordingly.

I use whole foods wherever possible. Sweet potatoes, dates and beans are my favourites. They require some preparing in advance, but it's well worth it, I promise! If you don't want to spend time cooking and blending your ingredients, then look out for the more straightforward recipes – they'll be in here too. You'll find that I repurpose some of the recipes from the "the basics" section to take your cake or cookies to the next level. I wanted to give you an idea of how you can integrate these into any baked good. If you don't have the time to make these in advance, you can use store-bought items. That said, it's worthwhile to go the extra mile and see how easy it is to make these yourself!

The recipes I've created in this book are a combination of nostalgic childhood treats and all-time favourites. Baking for me has always been about expressing my appreciation for the people I love, including myself. This book is a celebration of enjoying the treats you love without restriction, deprivation, or dieting. Life's too short, so you might as well make it sweet, right?

I love to see your creations so be sure to tag me on social media! @thathealthjunkie #thatsweetsweet

tips & tricks

get creative

If you don't have a specific ingredient on hand, check for substitutes. Make considered swaps with different fruits and nuts. For example, if peaches aren't in season, pick a fruit that is. If you can't find cashew butter, try almond or sunflower butter. You catch my drift? Don't feel restricted because there's always other options!

substitutions

Alternative flours have individual properties that react differently in baked goods. It's not as simple as swapping one flour for another. The same goes for sugars. If you decide to use a liquid sweetener instead of sugar crystals, you'll need to adjust the other liquid ingredients in the recipe. Double-check before you make any substitutions to see if they will work. Changing the chemistry of a recipe will give you a different result.

freeze

Buy and freeze fruits when they're in season and at their cheapest. By doing this, you will always have seasonal fruits on hand and can use them whenever you want. Some recipes (like dulce de leche or cookie dough) can be made in advance and stored in the freezer. When you need to use it for baking, simply let it thaw in the fridge.

buy

Some ingredients like dates, tahini and saffron, are more affordable in your local specialty shop. If you bake often, I recommend buying ingredients in larger quantities. Flours and sugars are cheaper when bought online in bulk. Make sure the suppliers have good quality ingredients - my favourite is Buy Whole Foods Online. This leads me to my next tip.

quality matters

While I encourage you to be savvy, buy the best quality you can afford. It makes a difference to the end result. That said, use what you can because it will all taste pretty damn good.

read first

Always read the recipe through before you start baking. When you know the steps beforehand, you avoid making silly mistakes - we've all been there!

temperature

Unless specified otherwise, ingredients should always be at room temperature. Whenever ingredients need to be chilled or melted, the recipe will mention it.

cup sizes

I use UK measuring cups in these recipes. UK cups are 250ml, whereas US cups are 240ml. If you're using a US cup, add an extra 2 teaspoons for every cup to get the same result.

repurpose

If you're missing a tool used in a recipe and you don't plan to use it again, I encourage you to repurpose what you already have. For example, use a long glass bottle or drinking glass instead of a rolling pin. Use a bottom of a crystal glass to make prints on your cookies or use the rim of a cup or a sharp round lid instead of a cookie cutter.

adjust

If you see that the recipe yields too much, you can divide it in half, quarters, or thirds. On the flip side, double the recipe if you want to make more. This easily applies to cookies, muffins and the "no bake" stuff, as all you need to do is double or divide the batter. To get the proportion right, make sure you're mathematically precise. For cakes, you will either need to split the batter between pans or use a larger baking pan. They might also need extra time in the oven. Start with the suggested time, and if it's not ready, check back every 5-10 minutes until done.

use your intuition

Yes, baking is a science and you should follow instructions to a T, but your equipment and kitchen climate may be different from mine. The brand or quality of your ingredients and even your oven will influence the end result.
If your cake batter or cookie dough doesn't match the recipe description, try and use your instincts to correct it. Batter too stiff? Add a bit of water. Cake browning too fast? Lower the oven temperature or reduce the cooking time.

use a timer

There's nothing worse than spending all that time baking only to end up with a burnt cake. Use a kitchen timer so that you won't forget you have something baking in the oven.

measure properly

To measure dry ingredients I use the dip and sweep method. First stir the flour to make sure it isn't compacted, dip the cup or spoon into the flour so it's overfilled, then use a straight knife to scrape the excess off the top. I always sift my flour *after* measuring. And I will mention this *just* in case - use proper measuring tools, please don't use ordinary spoons or glasses to measure!

be patient

When baking cakes, don't be tempted to open the oven door before it's done. Each time you do you let some of the heat out, which could cause the cake to collapse. Instead, use the oven light to check your cake's progress and try to keep the door closed until the baking time is completed.

storage

Make sure all baked goods have cooled completely before storing. Store them in an airtight container for up to 3-4 days at room temperature. If the recipe uses fresh frosting or whipped cream, then it's best stored in the fridge. Some of the bakes can be frozen in an airtight container or resealable bag for up to one month. Refer to each recipe for specific storage instructions.

don't waste

I always try to reduce food waste. If a recipe calls for one part of an egg, save the other part for another recipe, add it to your next meal, or freeze it for later use.
When the inevitable happens and things go wrong, get creative. Instead of throwing it out, repurpose it in something else. Unless it's fully burnt - don't eat burnt food.

serving

Heat it before you eat it. This is a personal preference as I'm a huge supporter of warm desserts - they just taste better!

wait to cool

This step is particularly important for cakes. You should wait for cakes to cool for at least 30 minutes before trying to remove them from the pan, otherwise you risk them falling apart.

ingredients

flour

oat flour 1:1 to regular flour
My most used flour. It's affordable, versatile and easy to work with. It has a soft, chewy texture. You can easily make your own by blending regular oats in a good food processor. While oats are naturally gluten-free, they can become tainted with gluten during processing. If you're sensitive to gluten, look for oats labelled as "gluten-free".

coconut flour 1:4 to regular flour
This flour is extremely absorbent and therefore has a drying effect on baked goods. It is made from dried coconut meat, which gives it a distinct flavour. When included in a recipe, it's important to add more liquid or eggs to avoid dry bakes. For good texture, it should be paired with other flours.

almond flour 1:1 to regular flour
Almond flour provides a mild, nutty taste and a delicate, soft texture. You can also use ground almonds, though they tend to be coarser and so you may need to use less liquid to reach the desired consistency. It is the priciest of alternative flours but one of the most versatile.

chickpea flour 1:1 to regular flour
A great binder, this flour is especially versatile in baking. Chickpea flour also adds a boost of protein to your bakes. Note that it shouldn't be used in raw desserts because it has an unpleasant legume-like taste when raw.

brown rice flour 1:1 to regular flour
While it has a subtly sweet, nutty flavour, it tends to make baked goods dry and crumbly but does well when combined with other flours, particularly in cookies. When choosing rice flour, try to look for a superfine variety as some flours can be a little gritty.

tapioca flour 2:1 to cornstarch
Also labelled as tapioca starch. It comes from the pulp of the cassava root. It's a great thickener for sauces and a binder for baking. It gives brownies and cookies a chewy texture, it also helps to imitate the stretchy dough consistency that gluten creates e.g. for cinnamon rolls (page 117).

sugar

coconut sugar 1:1 to refined sugar
This has a caramel-like flavour, similar to brown sugar.
It tends to darken batters so if you're concerned about the
appearance of your desserts and want it to look how it's
"supposed to" e.g. a light coloured sponge for lemon cake,
coconut sugar may not be the best option.

maple syrup ¾:1 to refined sugar
Maple syrup adds a delicious butterscotch flavour and tends
to darken baked goods. Whichever grade you use, make sure
it's not diluted with other refined syrups.

honey ⅔:1 to refined sugar
Always go for good quality, mild honey. You don't want the
taste to overpower your dessert. The baking temperature
should be lowered as honey tends to burn faster than other
sugars. Heat destroys most enzymes and nutrients in honey,
so the benefits of raw honey are only obtained from unbaked
desserts. I recommend buying local honey in bulk as it often
works out cheaper.

rapadura 1:1 to refined sugar
Rapadura (also called panela) is an unrefined sugar made from
evaporated cane juice. It has a caramel-like flavour, similar to
coconut sugar.

date sugar 1:⅔ to refined sugar
Although I haven't used date sugar in the recipes in this book,
it is one I highly recommend exploring. It's a lot less sweet
than other sugars. You can make your own by slow roasting
dates until hard and dry, then blend in a food processor until
fine.

date spread 1:1 to refined sugar
Not to be confused with date syrup, which is made by
straining dates and reducing into syrup. Date spread is simply
made by blending whole dates - this way all its nutrients are
retained (recipe on page 39). Because of its unique structure,
you might need to experiment a little if you want to use it to
substitute refined sugar.

fat

ghee
Ghee is my absolute favourite, it's made from pure butterfat (with the milk solids removed). Therefore, it's slightly more concentrated with vitamins and minerals. You can make your own (page 26). If you choose to buy it, make sure it doesn't have added oils or fillers.

butter
There's a reason why butter is a baker's best friend - the combination of the fat and moisture creates a tender texture and that classic home-baked taste. Always use unsalted butter to control the amount of salt in your bakes.

coconut oil
This is a great vegan substitute for butter. I recommend using extra virgin, cold-pressed coconut oil as it's more fragrant and contains more antioxidants.

cocoa butter
Cocoa butter is less used in baked goods but it's perfect for thinning chocolate or adding creaminess to a filling or coating. It's best combined with other fats like nut butter or coconut oil because the flavour can be overpowering.

tahini
I honestly didn't plan for there to be so many tahini recipes, but it just happened. It's an ingredient I can't go without and it's a must-try in baking. Made from ground sesame seeds, tahini has a nutty and slightly chocolatey taste. There is a slight bitterness to it and it works beautifully in sweet treats.

nut butter
All kinds of nut butter add great flavour and texture to baked goods. If possible, use 100% pure nut butter. In other words, one that is made exclusively from nuts with no added sugars, oils or preservatives.

coconut cream

This is my favourite dairy-free option for frosting cakes and cookies. Use full-fat coconut cream, without added gums or fillers. I've included guidance on how to prepare it (page 31). It can be used as a substitute for coconut yogurt.

coconut yogurt

As long as it's thick, this can be used interchangeably with coconut cream. My favourite brand is COYO; it's super creamy and not too tangy. If you're not a fan of coconut, use your preferred dairy-free yogurt.

other

cocoa & cacao powder

These both come from the cocoa bean. Cocoa powder is roasted at a high temperature, depleting some of its nutrients, whereas cacao powder is processed by cold-pressing, which makes it higher in antioxidants and flavonoids. Cocoa powder is darker in colour and sweeter to taste, whereas cacao powder is slightly more bitter - I like to use both.

leavening agents

Baking soda (bicarbonate of soda) is a base that reacts with acidic ingredients such as lemon juice or honey to expand and lighten the texture of baked goods. Baking powder is a complete leavening agent that contains baking soda, cream of tartar (an acid) and sometimes cornstarch. Double-acting (most common) reacts with both liquid and heat to create a rise. Use these interchangeably or together, as directed in recipes. Opt for aluminium-free, non-GMO baking powder.

milk

Choose any type of milk you like. Opt for ones without added thickeners, stabilisers and emulsifiers. My favourites are oat milk and coconut milk. You can easily make any dairy-free milk using a high-speed blender in a matter of minutes - it saves money and you know exactly what's inside!
If you prefer dairy milk, I recommend organic as the cows aren't given added hormones nor are they treated with antibiotics.

cinnamon

I prefer to use ground Ceylon or "true cinnamon", to cassia cinnamon. Ceylon has a more delicate, floral flavour and it's safer to consume in larger quantities. While cassia is perfectly safe in moderation, it shouldn't be consumed in high doses because it contains a compound, coumarin, that may cause health issues.

vanilla

There are many different forms of vanilla. I tend to use vanilla extract in most of my recipes as it's the most accessible. Opt for a high-quality vanilla extract, one that isn't made from artificial flavourings and chemicals. Ideally the ingredients should be: vanilla extract, alcohol and a small amount of sugar.

saffron

A kitchen staple in our household; saffron is a sweet and floral spice from a flower that adds a beautiful burst of colour to food. It's pricey but a little goes a long way. To prepare it, I grind batches in a pestle and mortar with a pinch of cane sugar to help grind it into a powder. Store it in a glass jar in the fridge. When adding it to recipes, add a pinch of saffron powder to hot water and let it steep for 5-15 minutes.

salt

Adding salt is a great way to bring out the flavours in desserts; it balances bitterness and sweetness. I alternate between using pure sea salt and Himalayan pink salt, as they both have beneficial minerals. If like me, you love that sweet and salty combination with some crunch, I recommend garnishing your desserts with salt flakes.

chocolate

You'll want good quality chocolate. In most of my recipes, I go for a cocoa content of 70% or more. If you don't like dark chocolate, you can use milk chocolate. I prefer to use chopped chocolate over chocolate chips. You can use either, as long as a recipe doesn't require the chocolate to be melted.

eggs

I alternate between medium and large eggs. I recommend using organic or pasture-raised eggs that come from chickens that roam around freely outside, with pesticide-free feed. If not, then free-range eggs will do just fine!

tools

food processor

You'll need one to make the cookie dough (page 35), to blend the chickpeas to a smooth consistency.

mini food chopper

Not essential but it's a great time saver for blending small amounts of ingredients and for chopping nuts - but yes, you can still chop nuts the old-fashioned way (with a knife).

rubber spatula

I highly recommend using one of these. They're affordable and great for scraping every last bit of batter from your mixing bowl. Waste not, want not!

angled palette knife

This is incredibly useful for smoothing cake and brownie batters, frostings, and fillings.

metal skewer

This is used to check the doneness of the cake. You can also use a toothpick or a small sharp knife.

electric whisk

Whether you use a hand or stand mixer, using an electric whisk is the best option for creaming sugars and fats or whipping up eggs. For most of the recipes, you can use a standard whisk instead but you'll need to double the whisking time. There are some recipes that you won't be able to make without an electric whisk, e.g. marshmallows (page 37).

candy thermometer

You'll need this to make sure the sugar reaches the right temperature when making the marshmallows (page 37).

parchment paper

There's nothing more frustrating than completely wrecking a bake while trying to remove it from the pan. Line your pans. For square cakes and bars, I recommend hanging some of the parchment over the edges. It's also helpful when rolling out dough. Opt for unbleached parchment paper.

baking pans & trays

For bars, brownies and some cakes, I use an 8-inch square baking pan as it's the perfect size for my household. If you use a larger baking pan (e.g. 12x9-inch), I recommend doubling up the recipe. If you don't want to make more, there's a more fussy option where you mould some parchment paper or foil to make a square inside the pan, then use an oven-proof utensil to keep the edges propped up - I used to do this all the time!

I use 8-inch round springform pans for cakes (page 97) springform is best, as they remove easily - less fuss! Sandwich cake pans work best for more runny batters that would leak through springform pans. For the "cookies n cream" cake (page 93), I use 7-inch sandwich pans. For the cookies I use large baking trays.

I use a standard size 12 cup muffin tin for muffins and "cups". They can be lined with cases or greased. You can also use silicone muffin moulds which I find easier for more delicate desserts like the "caramel cups" (page 147).

key

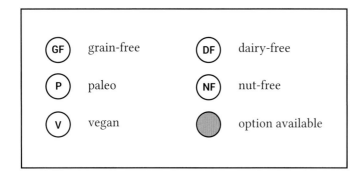

GF	grain-free	DF	dairy-free
P	paleo	NF	nut-free
V	vegan	●	option available

the basics

ghee

makes 24oz jar
prep time: 5 minutes
cook time: 30 minutes

Ghee is my kitchen staple. It tastes more buttery than butter and has a high smoke point. This means it's better suited for cooking at high temperatures, and won't burn as easily. It's shelf-stable and cheaper than the store-bought kind - an added bonus is that your house will smell amazing while making it!

750g /27oz unsalted butter

Place the butter in a large saucepan over medium heat and cook until melted. Turn the heat to low and allow to simmer uncovered for about 25-30 minutes.

Once the butter becomes fragrant and the middle layer turns from cloudy to clear, you'll see the milk solids have sunk to the bottom. That's when you know it's ready. You can now switch off the heat.

Place a small fine-mesh sieve over the opening of a sterilised glass jar and carefully pour in the ghee.

Allow to cool, put the lid on and place in the fridge to set.

Store an unopened jar in a cool, dark cupboard for up to nine months or in the fridge for up to a year. Opened jars can be stored at room temperature for about 3 months.

notes
I recommend using organic, grass-fed butter.

As an extra step, you can place a cheesecloth on top of the sieve in the straining process to ensure no milk solids go through.

When butter is turned into ghee, the milk solids are removed, therefore it is generally safe to consume if you're mildly lactose intolerant.

baked sweet potato

makes 1½ cups
prep time: 5 minutes
cook time: 50 minutes

This is one of my favourite baking ingredients. It's delicious on its own and also makes a great addition to desserts. The best way to bring out the sweetness of the sweet potato is by roasting them in the oven. This method can be used for Japanese white sweet potato, ube and purple sweet potato.

---

2 medium Japanese sweet potatoes

Preheat oven to 220°C /425°F/Gas 7 (200°C fan).

Wash the sweet potatoes and scrub if necessary. Use a fork to poke a few holes.

Place them on a baking tray and put in the middle of the oven to bake for 45-50 minutes. Check the doneness by inserting a knife into the centre. If it glides through, it should be ready. Allow them to cool, peel the skins and mash using a fork or potato masher until smooth.

Once mashed, measure and add the amount stated in the recipe and follow the instructions accordingly.

Store in the fridge for up to 4 days or freeze for up to 3 months.

notes

Adjust baking time according to the size of your sweet potatoes.

To freeze, measure the mashed sweet potato by either 1-cup or ½ cup sizes. This divides the potato into measurable pieces so they're ready for recipes. I like to bake a large batch of potatoes to have some readily available in the freezer. They also work great in smoothies and savoury dishes.

whipped coconut cream

makes 1 - 1½ cups
prep time: 10 minutes

1 can coconut cream
1-2 tbsp maple syrup
½ tsp vanilla extract

A dairy-free alternative cream for all your sweet treats - this is a great accompaniment for warm desserts or frosting a cake (page 93). Unwhipped coconut cream is often used in my recipes e.g. mint choc chunk bars (page 135). Here's some guidance on how to prepare it.

Chill a can of coconut cream overnight in the fridge to allow the cream to harden on top.

Before whipping, chill your mixing bowl in the freezer for 5-10 minutes. This isn't essential but it helps the cream whip up faster.

Remove the can from the fridge, making sure not to shake it as you want the cream to stay separated. Open the can and scoop the hardened cream off the top. You can save the liquid left behind for other recipes.

If you are preparing the cream to use as an ingredient for one of the recipes in this book and not as a frosting, you can stop here. Just measure and add the hardened cream to the recipe as instructed.

For whipped coconut cream, add the cream, maple syrup and vanilla extract to your mixing bowl and use an electric whisk to whip for 1-2 minutes until soft peaks form. If you find that the cream is too thick, stir in a bit of the liquid left behind in the can.

Serve the whipped cream as you wish, or store in an airtight container in the fridge for up to 1 week. When chilled, the cream will thicken more so give it another whisk when you are ready to use it.

notes

Some cans of coconut cream contain a higher cream to liquid ratio than others, so adjust the sweetness as needed.

Try finding a coconut cream without additives, as these don't allow for the cream and liquid to separate and the cream won't whip up. My go-to brand is Biona Organic.

You can also use a can of coconut milk, but this will likely contain less cream and more liquid. If this is the case, you may need to use more.

You can substitute the maple syrup for powdered sugar or stevia.

date spread

makes 8oz jar
soak time: 30 minutes +
prep time: 10 minutes

Not only are dates the most delicious fruit, but they are packed with nutrients. This is a simple way of turning dates into a spread, making it easy to add to recipes. My go-to varieties are Medjool, Bam and Bahri dates. Whichever one you go for, make sure they're moist.

---

2 packed cups pitted dates
1 tsp vanilla extract
pinch of salt

Place the dates in a large bowl and submerge in hot water for at least 30 minutes. If your dates are on the dry side, I recommend soaking them overnight or until they're super soft and squishy.

Drain the dates in a strainer and add along with the vanilla extract and salt to a food processor or high-speed blender. Blend on high while taking intervals to scrape down the sides. Keep going until it's smooth.

Scrape out into a jar and store in the fridge for up to a week or freeze for up to 3 months.

notes

If you don't have a blender or food processor, you can mash the dates using a fork. It won't be as smooth but you can still use it in recipes. You can also use a hand blender to make it smooth.

This can be used in place of the dulce de leche (page 45) in recipes - just add 4 tablespoons of milk for every cup of date spread to make it creamy.

cookie dough

makes 2 cups
prep time: 10 minutes

A satisfying treat that makes a great snack with a decent amount of protein. If you want to blend in a little extra liquid, it can be turned into a dip or frosting. It also makes a fun addition to other treats, like cookie dough nice cream (page 131) or cookie dough bites (page 145).

---

1 cup packed pitted dates
1½ cups chickpeas
¼ cup oat flour
2 tsp vanilla extract
¼ cup oat flour
⅓ cup cashew butter
1 tsp maca powder
¼ tsp baking soda
pinch of salt
1 cup chopped dark chocolate

Submerge the pitted dates with warm water and leave to soak for 1 hour.

Drain and rinse the dates and place all the ingredients, except for the chopped chocolate, in a food processor or a high-speed blender and blend until smooth.

Stir in the chopped chocolate until evenly distributed.

If you want to roll them into balls, wet your hands slightly to prevent the dough from sticking. Break off small pieces of cookie dough and roll into balls. If the mixture is too wet to handle, add a little extra oat flour.

Store in the fridge for up to 4 days or freeze for up to 3 months.

notes

Cashew butter can be substituted for almond or sunflower butter.

If your dates aren't moist, leave them to soak in water overnight.

If you want to use honey or maple syrup, add just a little at a time, as these are sweeter than dates.

To make a dip or frosting: blend in some milk to reach desired consistency, before adding the chocolate chunks.

To freeze in advance, measure by either 1 cup or ½ cup sizes and divide the cookie dough into measurable pieces so they're ready for future recipes.

marshmallows

makes 25 squares
prep time: 15 minutes
cook time: 10 minutes
setting time: 6 hours

ghee or oil for greasing
½ cup warm water, divided
1½ tbsp powdered gelatine
½ cup light honey
1 tsp vanilla extract
tapioca flour for dusting

I'm so excited to share this recipe with you! Turn honey and gelatine into squishy, sweet fluffy clouds, like magic. Not to mention the deep satisfaction you will feel once you make your own *and* you get to make all the s'mores you ever wanted!

Line an 8-inch square baking pan with parchment paper, lightly grease the paper and sprinkle tapioca flour over the base until mostly covered.

Grease a spatula and sharp knife to prevent sticking and set aside.

Mix the gelatine and ¼ cup warm water in a large bowl and set aside.

Put the honey and the remaining ¼ cup of water in a saucepan over medium-high heat until it comes to a gentle boil. Cover the saucepan, lower the heat and allow to simmer for 3 minutes.

After 3 minutes, lift the lid and place a thermometer inside the saucepan. Once it reaches 118°C/ 244°F begin the next step, as the honey mixture is ready.

Beat the gelatine-water mixture with an electric whisk on low. Slowly pour the heated honey-water mixture down the side of the bowl to avoid burning the gelatine. Add vanilla extract and continue to whisk for 5-8 minutes until the marshmallow mixture triples in size and is thick, fluffy and shiny. Do not to stop whisking until you reach this stage.

Scrape the mix into the prepared baking pan and spread evenly using an oiled spatula. Use a sieve to generously dust the top with tapioca flour and cover the pan with cling film. Allow to set for at least 6 hours.

With the greased knife, cut the marshmallow into squares. Toss each cube in tapioca flour.

Store in an airtight container at room temperature for up to 5 days.

notes

This can be a sensitive recipe because of timing and temperature, therefore make sure you follow the steps to get the desired results.

For mini marshmallows, slice into smaller, ½ inch squares.

Dusting with tapioca flour is a necessary step for the marshmallows to set. It also helps prevent them from turning clear when they're heated.

Opt for high-quality, grass-fed gelatine - I use Great-Lakes.

vanilla custard

makes 580 ml jar
prep time: 5 minutes
cook time: 20 minutes

Cake and custard was a real treat I had growing up, especially at school. I would sometimes use my lunch money to buy two puddings and skip on the main - I know. Here's a recipe for a silky-smooth vanilla custard that reminds me of sweet childhood memories. Make this to serve with warm cake or a fruity crumble.

---

1 vanilla pod
3 medium egg yolks
2 tbsp tapioca flour
3 tbsp maple syrup
2 cups milk of choice

Using a sharp knife, split the vanilla pod lengthways down the middle and scrape out the seeds. Pour the milk into a small saucepan, add the pod and seeds. Cook over medium-low heat until it starts to bubble.

Take the pan off the heat and leave to cool slightly. Once cooled, remove the vanilla pod.

In a medium bowl, whisk the egg yolks, maple syrup and tapioca flour until it's lump-free and well combined.

Gradually add the warm milk to the egg yolks while whisking until well combined.

Pour the mixture back into the saucepan and cook over low heat while continuously whisking for 15-20 minutes or until thickened. Pour over your favourite dessert and enjoy!

(P) (DF) (NF) (GF)

notes

If the egg starts to scramble, don't worry. Simply allow the custard to cool slightly, then use a hand blender to blend until smooth. Alternatively, strain through a sieve to remove any lumps.

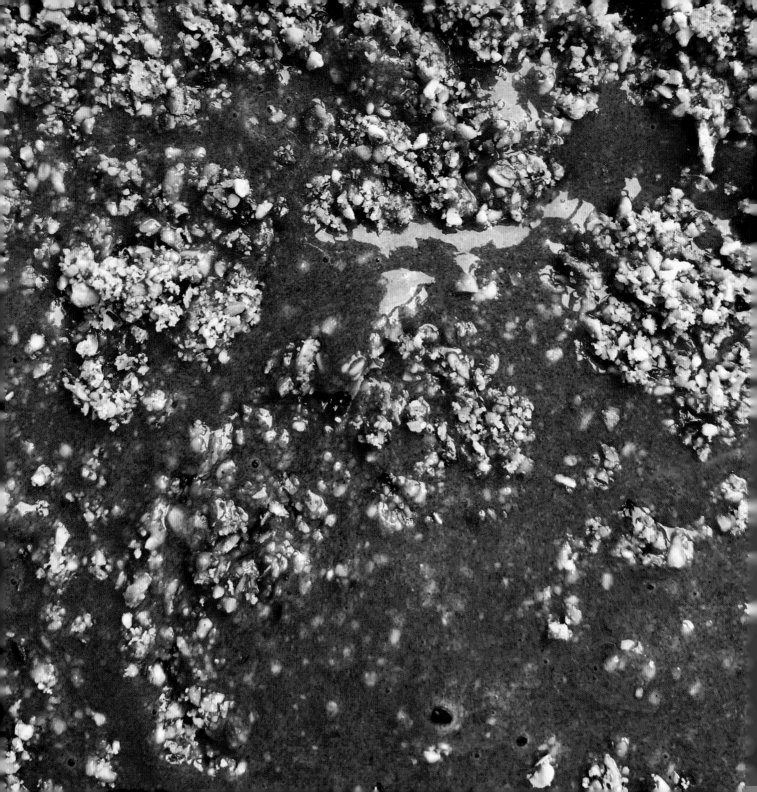

halva spread

makes 8oz jar
prep time: 5 minutes
cook time: 5 minutes

If you still think tahini is only good for hummus, then think again. Sweetened tahini is life changing. This recipe makes a great breakfast spread as well as a delicious addition to desserts. You can swirl it into brownies, drizzle it on cakes or even top your smoothies with it.

⅓ cup shelled pistachios
¾ cup tahini
2 tbsp coconut oil
¼ cup date syrup
1 tsp vanilla extract
pinch of salt

Place the pistachios in a small frying pan over medium heat and toast for about 5 minutes while continuously stirring to avoid burning. Once fragrant and slightly browned, take it off the heat and allow to cool.

Pulse the pistachios in a food processor until ground and powdery.

Place the tahini, coconut oil and date syrup in a small saucepan over medium-low heat. Whisk until the coconut oil has melted and the ingredients are combined, then take off the heat. Mix in the ground pistachios, vanilla extract and salt, and stir to combine.

Pour into an airtight glass jar and store in the fridge for up to 2 weeks.

notes

The spread will harden when it's cold. To liquify, remove the lid and submerge the bottom half of the jar in a pot of a couple inches of water. Gently heat and stir until drizzly.

If you don't have date syrup, you can use date spread (page 33) or maple syrup instead.

If you choose to use salted roasted pistachios, leave the salt out of this recipe.

strawberry chia jam

makes 8oz jar
prep time: 5 minutes
cook time: 20 minutes

Strawberry jam was the only flavoured jam I liked as a kid and I can still see why. Not only is it good on toast, but it can be added to other desserts like pb&j crumb bites (page 77) and shortbread delights (page 59). My version of this breakfast staple comes with the added benefits of nutrient-packed chia seeds.

3 cups chopped strawberries
2 tbsp chia seeds
2 tbsp maple syrup

Place the strawberries in a saucepan and mash with a potato masher to your desired consistency. Alternatively, use a hand blender or place the strawberries in a food processor and pulse until smooth. Simmer over medium heat for about 20 minutes while stirring occasionally. Take the strawberries off the heat and stir in the chia seeds and maple syrup.

Pour into a glass jar and allow to cool. Screw the lid on and store in the fridge for up to 1 week or freeze for up to 3 months.

(P) (DF) (NF) (GF) (V)

notes
If you prefer for it to be extra smooth, you can blend it after it has cooled.

The sweetness of the strawberries may vary so adjust the maple syrup accordingly.

dulce de leche

makes 16 bars
prep time: 10 minutes
cook time: 25 minutes

1 cup mashed
Japanese sweet
potatoes (page 29)
⅓ cup coconut sugar
2 tbsp ghee
2 tbsp milk
½ tsp vanilla extract
pinch of salt

When I was 10 my auntie brought back a jar of dulce de leche from Argentina and I've been obsessed ever since. Here is my take on it. It's incredibly decadent and moreish. The spread makes a great addition to desserts, as well as breakfasts. Enjoy on pancakes, porridge, toast, anything you like.

Add the sweet potato, coconut sugar and ghee to a food processor or high-speed blender and blend until smooth. Scrape down the sides and add the milk, vanilla extract and salt. Blend until smooth.

Transfer to a glass jar, screw on the lid and store in the fridge for up to 1 week or in the freezer for up to 3 months.

notes
Make it vegan-friendly by replacing ghee with coconut oil.

To freeze in advance, measure by either 1 cup or ½ cup sizes and divide the dulce de leche into measurable pieces so they're ready for future recipes.

cookies

white chunk macadamia cookies

makes 20 cookies
prep time: 15 minutes
cook time: 10 minutes
chill time: overnight

1¼ cups brown rice flour
2 tbsp tapioca flour
1 tsp baking soda
½ tsp baking powder
¼ tsp salt
⅓ cup light honey
1 medium egg, beaten
½ cup melted butter
1 tsp vanilla extract
½ cup chopped white chocolate
½ cup chopped macadamia nuts

These take me back to times when I used to go to the US as a kid and I'd get white chocolate macadamia nut cookies from the Great American Cookie Co at the mall. For these soft-baked cookies, I used rice flour which gives them a slightly crumbly texture and a delicate, nutty flavour.

Sift and combine the flours, baking soda, baking powder and salt in a large bowl. Make a well in the centre of the dry mix and add the honey, egg, butter and vanilla extract. Mix with a spatula until just combined. Add the chopped white chocolate and nuts and stir until evenly distributed. The cookie dough should be a little looser than regular cookie dough.

Chill the cookie dough overnight (this enhances both the flavour and texture).

Take the cookie dough out of the fridge for about an hour to soften.

Preheat the oven to 200°C/400°F/Gas 6 (180°C fan). Line two baking trays with parchment paper.

Use a medium cookie scoop to place the dough balls onto the trays. Leave about a 4-inch gap between each cookie.

Place the tray in the middle of the oven to bake for a total of 8-10 minutes. After 5 minutes of baking, take the cookies out the oven and gently tap the tray against a hard surface until it creates cracks on the surface. Place the tray back in the oven to finish baking for another 3-5 minutes or until the edges are lightly golden.

Leave the cookies to cool on the trays for 10 minutes, then transfer to a cooling rack to cool completely.

notes

If you can't chill the cookie dough overnight, I recommend chilling for at least 30 minutes to help it develop a richer flavour.

If you want your cookies to spread, leave the cookie dough out to reach room temperature before baking.

Don't leave out the white chocolate chunks as they contribute to the overall sweetness of the cookie.

chocolate caramel rounds

makes 26 cookies
prep time: 25 minutes
bake time: 20 minutes
setting time: 1 hour

These remind me of the biscuit bars I used to have as an after-school snack. It's got all the goods packed into one cookie: a crumbly base, topped with a thick layer of dulce de leche and covered in chocolate. Welcome to paradise.

---

cookie
1 cup almond flour
1 cup oat flour
¼ cup coconut sugar
½ tsp baking soda
¼ cup softened butter
1 medium egg, whisked
1 tsp vanilla extract

filling
1 cup dulce de leche
(page 45)
1 cup finely chopped
dark chocolate
bee pollen, to decorate

Preheat the oven to 200°C/400°F/Gas 6 (180°C fan) and line a baking tray with parchment paper.

Sift and combine the flours in a large bowl. Add the coconut sugar, baking soda, butter, egg and vanilla extract and mix until a dough forms.

Using a rolling pin, roll out the dough on a floured surface to a thickness of about ¼ inch. Use a 2-inch cookie cutter to cut out as many cookies as you can. Place the cookies on the tray. Gather the dough scraps, roll out and repeat until all the dough is used.

Place the tray in the middle of the oven and bake for 15-18 minutes or until golden brown. Leave the cookies in the tray to cool completely.

Once cooled, add about 1 tablespoon of dulce de leche to each cookie and spread it evenly with an angled palette knife. Transfer the cookies to the freezer to set for 1 hour.

Fill a saucepan with 2 inches of water and bring to a simmer. Place a heat-proof bowl over a saucepan, making sure it fits snugly. Add the chopped chocolate to the bowl and stir until all the chocolate has melted. Remove from the heat and set aside.

Carefully dip each cookie into the melted chocolate until fully coated and use a fork to place it on a cooling rack.

Sprinkle with bee pollen and transfer to the fridge to set.

Store in the fridge for 3-4 days or in the freezer in an airtight container for up to 3 months.

---

notes
Allow them to sit at room temperature for at least 1 hour before serving, so the centre will be soft and velvety.

To make it grain-free, substitute the oat flour for an extra cup of almond flour.

s'mores cookies

makes 12 cookies
prep time: 15 minutes
cook time: 12 minutes

I used to stock up on graham crackers every time I went to the US, just so I could make s'mores back at home. The combination of a cracker, toasted marshmallow and melty chocolate is everything. This is not only a more practical way to enjoy s'mores, but there ain't nothing more satisfying than biting into a warm cookie with a gooey marshmallow centre.

¼ cup coconut sugar
⅓ cup melted ghee
1 medium egg
½ tsp vanilla extract
1¼ cup almond flour
½ cup tapioca flour
½ tsp baking powder
⅛ tsp salt
½ cup chopped dark chocolate
12 marshmallows (page 37)

Preheat the oven to 200°C/400°F/Gas 6 (180°C fan) and line two baking trays with parchment paper.

Whisk the coconut sugar, ghee, egg and vanilla extract with an electric whisk on high speed for 3 minutes.

Sift in the flours, baking powder and salt and fold until a cookie dough is formed. Add the dark chocolate and fold again until just combined.

Push some cookie dough into a cookie scoop, making sure that the base of the scoop is fully covered. Add a marshmallow cube to the base, then use another piece of cookie dough to enclose the marshmallow inside.

Carefully release the lever of the cookie scoop over the baking tray, leaving a 4-inch gap between each cookie. Place the tray in the middle of the oven and bake for 8-12 minutes or until lightly golden on top.

---

notes

Most of the sweetness comes from the marshmallow. If you don't want to use marshmallows, I suggest adding something else that will add the same amount of sweetness, like dulce de leche (page 45), white chocolate or strawberry chia jam (page 43).

cookie dough whoopie pies

makes 10 whoopie pies
prep time: 20 minutes
cook time: 14 minutes

These cookie dough whoopie pies consist of soft and airy cocoa cookies filled with gooey chocolate chip cookie dough (page 35). Undoubtedly, a satisfying treat with a combination that your tastebuds don't want to miss!

---

cookie
¼ cup oat flour
¼ cup tapioca flour
1 tbsp cocoa powder
½ tsp baking powder
¾ cup chopped dark chocolate
2 tbsp butter
½ cup coconut sugar
1 large egg
½ tsp vanilla extract
¼ tsp salt

filling
½ cup cookie dough (page 35)
3 tbsp chopped dark chocolate (optional)

Preheat the oven to 200°C/400°F/Gas 6 (180°C fan) and line two baking trays with parchment paper.

In a medium bowl, sift the flours, cocoa powder, baking powder, and salt. Mix and set aside.

Fill a saucepan with 2 inches of water and bring to a simmer. Place a heat-proof bowl over a saucepan, making sure it fits snugly. Add ¾ cup chopped chocolate and butter to the bowl and stir until all the chocolate has melted. Remove from the heat and set aside to cool.

Whisk the coconut sugar, egg, and vanilla extract in a large bowl on medium speed for 5 minutes. Reduce the speed to low, add the melted chocolate and beat for 1 minute. Add the flour mixture and mix on a low speed until just combined. It should look like brownie batter.

Use a cookie scoop lightly coated with non-stick spray. Scoop the batter onto the baking trays, leaving a 4-inch gap between each one.

Place the baking tray in the middle of the oven and bake for 12-14 minutes, until the tops are shiny. Let them cool in the tray for 10 minutes. Transfer the cookies to a cooling rack to cool completely.

Add about ¾ tablespoons of cookie dough to the underside of half the cookies and top with the other half to make your whoopie pie. Roll the finished whoopie pies in chopped dark chocolate.

Store in an airtight container in the fridge for up to 5 days.

notes
No cookie dough? No problem. You can enjoy these sandwiched with a more classic whipped cream filling, ice cream or even dulce de leche.

pistachio cookie cups

makes 12 cookie cups
prep time: 25 minutes
cook time: 12 minutes

I love pistachio flavoured desserts because they are indulgent, yet still light and fragrant. These cookie cups serve you double pistachio trouble with a crumbly pistachio cookie conveniently shaped in a cup to hold a creamy pistachio filling - a beaut.

cookie cup
2 tbsp ghee, plus extra for greasing
1 cup almond flour
½ tsp baking soda
pinch of salt
1 medium egg
¼ cup maple syrup
6 tbsp pistachio butter

filling
½ cup coconut cream (page 31)
6 tbsp pistachio butter
¼ cup maple syrup
1 tsp vanilla extract

ground pistachios to decorate

Preheat the oven to 200°C/400°F/Gas 6 (180°C fan) and grease a standard-size 12-cup muffin pan.

Mix the almond flour, baking soda and salt to a large bowl and set aside. In another bowl, whisk the egg, maple syrup, ghee and pistachio butter.

Add the egg mixture to the flour and gently fold with a spatula until just combined.

Divide the dough into 12 balls, flatten slightly in your hands and place in the muffin mould. Press down until the centre is indented and the edges are raised.

Place the muffin pan in the middle of the oven and bake for 8-12 minutes.

In the meantime, prepare the filling. Add the coconut cream, pistachio butter, maple syrup and vanilla extract to a medium mixing bowl and whisk until well combined.

Remove the cookie cups from the oven. The base of the cookie cup may have risen while baking, so use the back of a teaspoon, or another rounded utensil, to flatten the base again.

Once the cookies have cooled, divide the filling equally between the cookie cups and sprinkle ground pistachio on top to decorate.

Store in an airtight container in the fridge for 3-4 days.

notes
Coconut cream can be substituted for coconut yogurt or dairy cream.

If you don't have pistachio butter, you can make your own by blending pistachios in a high-speed blender or food processor until smooth and creamy.

To make ground pistachio, blend in a mini food chopper or food processor or chop it finely with a sharp knife and set aside.

shortbread delights

makes 18 cookies
prep time: 30 minutes
cook time: 10 minutes
chill time: 20 minutes

I loved Viennese whirls - the tender shortbread combined with a fruity filling is next level. These delights remind me of them. They are made with two layers of soft crumbly cookie, layered with both a sweet and creamy filling. They make a fancy treat for a gathering or an afternoon tea with friends.

cookie
1 cup oat flour
1 cup brown rice flour
¼ cup light honey
½ cup ghee, at room temperature
1 tsp vanilla extract

filling
3 tbsp coconut yogurt
3 tbsp strawberry chia jam (page 43)

Sift and combine the flours in a large bowl and set aside. In another bowl, whisk the honey, ghee and vanilla extract until well combined.

Using a spatula, slowly fold the wet ingredients into the flour mixture until just incorporated. Do not overmix.

Preheat the oven to 200°C/400°F/Gas 6 (180°C fan). Line two baking trays with parchment paper.

Working on a floured surface, use a rolling pin to roll out the dough to a thickness of about ¼ inch. Use a 2-inch fluted-edge cookie cutter and cut out about 18 cookies. Place them on the baking trays leaving a gap between each cookie. Gather the dough scraps, roll out and repeat until all the dough is used. Transfer the trays to the fridge and chill for 20 minutes. This will help them keep their shape while baking.

Place in the middle of the oven to bake for 10 minutes or until slightly golden around the edges. Leave the cookies to rest for 10 minutes then transfer to a cooling rack to cool completely.

Once cooled, the cookies are ready to fill. Flip the cookies upside down and place ½ teaspoon coconut yogurt to the centre of half of the cookies. Spread the filling, leaving a small gap around the edges. Repeat the process with the remaining cookies using ½ teaspoon of chia jam on each. Once they're all covered, gently sandwich one yogurt and one jam-covered cookie together.

Store in an airtight container in the fridge for 3-4 days.

notes
If you prefer, you can swap coconut yogurt for cream or another thick dairy-free yogurt.
You can skip chilling the dough if you're short on time.
These are best eaten on the day they are filled, as the strawberry chia jam tends to run into the coconut yogurt so they won't look *as* neat.

noreos

makes 16 cookies
prep time: 40 minutes
cook time: 10 minutes
setting time: 10 minutes

Noreo's - *not* Oreo's but pretty damn close. These are made with a coconut butter filling so there's a subtle uniqueness to the traditional sandwich cookie. I'm always so excited to create anything flavoured 'cookies n cream' – and these babies are perfect for that purpose. Add them to brownies, cheesecake and frosting for cakes (my fave).

cookie
⅔ cup coconut sugar
¼ cup coconut oil
1 large egg
½ cup cocoa powder
¼ cup tapioca flour
½ cup oat flour
1 tsp vanilla extract

filling
8 tbsp melted coconut butter
2 tbsp maple syrup
½ tsp vanilla extract

Preheat oven 200°C/400°F/Gas 6 (180°C fan) and line a large baking tray with parchment paper.

Combine all the cookie ingredients together in a bowl, mixing until a dough forms. Working on a floured surface, use a rolling pin to roll out the dough to a thickness of about ¼ inch.

Use a patterned cookie stamp to imprint the dough as many times as you can. Then, using a 2-inch round cookie cutter, cut out the circles and carefully transfer to the baking tray. Gather the dough scraps, roll out and repeat until all the dough is used.

Bake for 8-10 minutes. Once out of the oven, leave the cookies on the tray to cool completely.

In the meantime, prepare the filling. Mix the coconut butter, maple syrup and vanilla extract in a small bowl until well combined. Once the cookies have cooled, add a teaspoon of the filling to the centre of each and gently press down using a second cookie. Transfer the filled cookies to the fridge and leave to set. Store in an airtight container at room temperature for 3-4 days or freeze for up to 3 months.

notes

You can use a patterned rolling pin to make an imprint on the dough instead of a cookie stamp.

If the dough is on the dry side, add water half a teaspoon at a time, until it's easy to roll out.

caramel cookies

makes 12 cookies
prep time: 40 minutes
cook time: 15 minutes

½ cup coconut sugar
½ cup softened butter
1 medium egg
1 tsp vanilla extract
1½ cup chickpea flour
2 tbsp tapioca flour
1 tsp baking soda
1 tsp baking powder
pinch of salt
⅓ cup chopped dark chocolate

6 tbsp chilled dulce de leche (page 45)

What's not to like about these cookies?! They have a slightly crisp exterior with a soft caramelly centre. Just lovely.

Preheat the oven to 180°C/350°F/Gas 4 (160°C fan). Line a couple baking trays with parchment paper and set aside.

Using an electric whisk, cream the sugar and butter for 2-3 minutes or until it's light and fluffy. Add the egg and vanilla and whisk for another 2 minutes.

Sift in the flours, baking soda, baking powder and salt, fold until combined. Fold in the chopped chocolate.

As an option, you can chill the dough for an hour.

Push some cookie dough into a cookie scoop, making sure that the base of the scoop is fully covered. Add about ½ tablespoon dulce de leche. Get another piece of cookie dough and flatten, then gently press on top of the scoop to enclose the edges.

Carefully release the lever of the cookie scoop over the baking tray, leaving a 4-inch gap between each cookie. Place the tray in the middle of the oven and bake for 12-14 minutes or until lightly golden on top.

notes

If you choose to makes these without the caramel in the middle, add an extra ¼ to ½ cup of sugar to the mixture to compensate for the sweetness.

Make sure the cookies are cooked through as when chickpea flour is undercooked, it tends to taste legumey - if this happens, put them back in the oven to bake for another 5 minutes.

persimmon thumbprints

makes 20 thumbprints
prep time: 15 minutes
cook time: 15 minutes

A classic treat to make for the holidays and they're also fun to make! These cookies have a soft airy base, filled with a caramel-like persimmon jelly.

cookies
¾ cup oat flour
½ cup almond flour
1 tsp cinnamon
pinch of salt
¼ cup melted
coconut oil
¼ cup light honey
¾ tsp vanilla extract

persimmon jelly
1 large very ripe
Hachiya persimmon
1 tsp tapioca flour
½ tsp vanilla extract

Preheat the oven to 180°C/350°F/Gas 4 (160°C fan). Line a couple baking trays with parchment paper and set aside.

Sift and combine the flours, cinnamon and salt in a large bowl. Add the coconut oil, honey, vanilla extract and fold with a spatula until a dough forms.

Divide the dough into about 20 pieces and roll into balls. Place them on the tray, making sure they're evenly spaced. Use your thumb or the end of a thick, rounded utensil to slowly press into the centre of each cookie.

Place the tray in the centre of the oven and bake for 12-15 minutes until golden around the edges.

Once the cookies are out the oven, the centres will have risen a little. Gently press them back down and set aside to cool completely.

To make the persimmon jelly remove the top of the persimmon and peel the skin. Chop the persimmon into cubes and put inside the mini food chopper or a high-speed blender. Add tapioca flour and vanilla extract and blend until smooth. Transfer to a small saucepan and cook over medium-low heat and stir until thickened, about 5 minutes. If it gets a little lumpy, you can place the jelly back in the blender and blend until smooth.

Once the cookies have cooled, spoon the persimmon jelly into each dent. Store in an airtight container in the fridge for up to 4 days.

notes

You want the persimmon to be very ripe, the inside should resemble jam. If your persimmon is seeded, make sure to remove the seeds first.

As persimmons are seasonal, you can make a similar filling with another ripened fruit of choice. Or you can try the strawberry chia jam (page 43), halva spread (page 41) or your favourite nut butter.

For a vegan option, substitute honey for maple syrup or your preferred liquid sweetener.

chocolate hazelnut sandwich cookies

makes 14 cookies
prep time: 25 minutes
cook time: 12 minutes

I'm a big advocate for hazelnut desserts, especially when they're creamy and *especially* when there's chocolate involved. These pillowy hazelnut cookies are filled with a thick chocolate hazelnut filling and each bite is a real delight.

cookie
½ cup hazelnut butter
½ cup coconut sugar
¼ cup water
½ tsp vanilla extract
½ cup almond flour
¼ cup tapioca flour
½ tsp baking soda
½ tsp baking powder
pinch of salt

hazelnut creme
½ cup coconut yogurt
½ cup hazelnut butter
2 tbsp cacao powder
2 tbsp maple syrup

Preheat the oven to 200°C/400°F/Gas 6 (180°C fan). Line two baking trays with parchment paper.

Add the hazelnut butter and coconut sugar to a large bowl. Use an electric whisk to whisk the mixture on high speed for 1 minute. Add the water and vanilla extract and whisk until well combined. Sift in the flours, baking soda, baking powder and salt and fold until combined. Use a teaspoon to divide the dough into 14 equal parts. Roll into small balls and place on the tray, leaving a 2-inch gap between each cookie. Place the baking tray in the middle of the oven and bake for 10-12 minutes. Leave the cookies on the tray to cool completely.

In the meantime, prepare the hazelnut creme. Add the coconut yogurt, hazelnut butter, cocoa powder and maple syrup to a small bowl and mix until well combined. Once the cookies have cooled completely, spread about 1 tbsp of the hazelnut creme on the underside of a cookie. Use another cookie to sandwich them together. Repeat with the remaining cookies and hazelnut creme.

Store them in an airtight container in the fridge for up to 4 days.

notes
These are best served soon after assembling. The cookies will soften from the filling when stored, however, they'll still be delicious.

You can also bake the cookies and hazelnut creme in advance and assemble right before serving.

bars

hazelnut swirl brownies

makes 16 bars
prep time: 10 minutes
cook time: 25 minutes

These bars are somewhat of a hybrid between a blondie and a brownie. The effort is minimal as you don't need two separate batters - fancy, without the trouble. These are dense, chewy and absolutely delicious.

blondie
¾ cup hazelnut butter
2 tbsp ghee
¾ cup coconut sugar
1 tsp vanilla extract
3 medium eggs
1½ tbsp tapioca flour
⅓ cup coconut flour
pinch of salt

brownie
⅓ cup cacao powder
½ tbsp water

Preheat the oven to 200°C/400°F/Gas 6 (180°C fan). Grease an 8-inch square baking pan and line with parchment paper.

In a large bowl, whisk together the hazelnut butter, ghee and coconut sugar with an electric whisk for 2 minutes. Add the vanilla extract and eggs one at a time, whisking after each addition. Sift in the flours and salt and fold until just combined.

Divide the batter equally into two bowls. Add the cacao powder and water to one of the bowls and stir to combine.

Pour half of the blondie batter into the baking pan. Add spoonfuls of the brownie batter, making sure they're evenly spaced. Spoon the remaining blondie batter on top. Use a sharp knife to create swirls through the batter.

Place the baking pan in the middle of the oven and bake for 20-25 minutes or until the blondie section turns golden. Take the pan out the oven and allow to cool completely before slicing.

Store in an airtight container at room temperature for up to 4 days.

notes
Skip the cacao powder and water for plain hazelnut blondies.

peaches n cream blondies

makes 16 bars
prep time: 10 minutes
cook time: 25 minutes

When summer comes around, you gotta make the most out of those peaches! These blondies do great justice to the classic peaches 'n cream duo. Here you have blondies layered with juicy peaches and sweetened cream cheese swirled in.

ghee or oil for greasing

cream
½ cup cream cheese
2 tbsp light honey
1 tsp vanilla extract
1 tsp tapioca flour

blondies
¼ cup honey
2 medium eggs
⅓ cup cashew butter
½ tsp vanilla extract
1 cup almond flour
pinch of salt

1 cup finely diced and drained ripe peaches

Preheat the oven to 200°C/400°F/Gas 6 (180°C fan). Grease an 8-inch square baking pan and line with parchment paper.

Whisk the ingredients for the cream to come together in a medium bowl and set aside.

In a large bowl, whisk the honey, eggs, cashew butter and vanilla extract until smooth. Add the almond flour and salt and fold with a rubber spatula until combined.

Pour ¾ of the blondie batter into the baking pan.

Add spoonfuls of the cream mixture on top, making sure they're evenly spaced. Do the same with the peaches. Finish by adding the remaining blondie batter. Use a sharp knife to create swirls throughout the batter.

Place the pan in the middle of the oven and bake for 20-25 minutes or until the top starts to brown. Remove from the oven and leave the blondies in the pan to cool completely before slicing into squares.

Store in an airtight container in the fridge for up to 4 days.

notes

The tapioca flour can be substituted with 2 teaspoons of cornstarch.

If you don't have cashew butter, use almond or sunflower butter.

Some almond flours are finer than others, if your batter is too thick, add 1 tablespoon of water at a time until it reaches the same consistency as the cream mixture.

If peaches aren't in season, you can use other fruits. Ripe persimmons work well in this recipe.

s'mores crumb bars

makes 12 bars
prep time: 10 minutes
cook time: 12 minutes

You don't need a campfire to enjoy these buttery, gooey bars. Loaded with toasted marshmallows and melted chocolate, they're a lot easier to make and slightly less messy to eat than traditional s'mores.

¼ cup ghee, plus extra for greasing
1½ cups oat flour
¼ cup coconut sugar
1 tsp vanilla extract
pinch of salt
⅓ cup chopped dark chocolate
2 cups marshmallows (page 37)

Preheat the oven to 200°C/400°F/Gas 6 (180°C fan). Grease an 8-inch square baking pan and line with the parchment paper, making sure that it hangs over the edges.

Place the oat flour, ghee, coconut sugar and vanilla extract in a large bowl. Use your fingers to rub the ingredients until the crumbs clump into coarse pieces.

Press ¾ of the crumb mixture into the pan. Place in the middle of the oven and bake for 12 minutes. Scatter the chocolate and marshmallows evenly over the base then finish by crumbling the remaining crumb mixture on top.

Put the pan back in the oven and bake for 8-12 minutes or until the marshmallows turn golden brown. Leave the bars in the pan to cool for an hour. Slice into squares and serve.

Store in an airtight container at room temperature for 4-5 days.

notes

If you like a more oaty texture, go half and half with whole oats and oat flour.

The parchment paper makes it easier to remove the bars from the pan, as the marshmallows tend to get super sticky.

To make this dairy-free and vegan, substitute the ghee for coconut oil and use vegan marshmallows.

pb&j crumb bites

makes 16 bites
prep time: 10 minutes
cook time: 40 minutes

Once you've had your first bite you'll find it hard to stop. The sweet, fruity filling perfectly balances out the rich, crumbly oats in the bars. It's a great bring-a-dish recipe as it's quick to make and easy to transport. Not to mention they're delicious and seriously addictive.

---

ghee or oil for greasing
2 cups oat flour
½ cup coconut sugar
1 cup roasted peanut butter
1 tsp vanilla extract
¼ cup water
½ cup strawberry chia jam (page 43)
½ cup chopped strawberries

Preheat the oven to 200°C/400°F/Gas 6 (180°C fan). Grease an 8-inch square baking pan and line with parchment paper.

Place the oat flour, coconut sugar, peanut butter and vanilla extract in a large bowl. Use your fingers to rub the mixture together until it starts to resemble small crumbs. Add the water and continue mixing with your hands until the crumbs clump together.

Press about ¾ of the oat mixture into the pan. Add the jam and smooth over with a spatula.

Sprinkle the strawberries evenly on top, and finish by crumbling over the remaining ¼ oat mixture.

Place in the middle of the oven to bake for 35-40 minutes, until the crumble is lightly golden. Leave the bars in the pan to cool completely before slicing into squares.

Store in an airtight container in the fridge for 3-4 days.

---

notes
You can use whole oats and blitz them in a food processor to break them down to your preferred texture.

If you find the crumble too dry, add water 1 tablespoon at a time until it comes together to a crumble-like consistency.

pecan maple blondies

makes 12 blondies
prep time: 10 minutes
cook time: 30 minutes

ghee or oil for greasing
½ cup cashew butter
½ cup pure grade A
maple syrup
1 cup pecan halves,
extra for topping
2 large eggs
3 tbsp coconut flour
⅛ teaspoon salt

There was a time where I was addicted to pecan maple plaits. I'd get them after school and heat them in the oven, which would leave the house smelling of its sweet sweet scent. So here they are in the form of a blondie.

Preheat the oven to 200°C/400°F/Gas 6 (180°C fan). Grease an 8-inch square baking pan and line with parchment paper.

Place the cashew butter, maple syrup and pecan halves in a high-speed blender (or food processor) and blend until the pecans are mostly ground up.

Add the eggs one at a time, blending between each addition. Finally, add the coconut flour and salt and blend until just combined.

Pour into the pan and sprinkle a handful of pecans on top. Place the pan in the middle of the oven and bake for 25-30 minutes, until the top is lightly golden. Leave the blondies in the pan to cool completely before slicing into squares.

Store in an airtight container in the fridge for 4-5 days.

notes

The cashew butter can be replaced with almond or sunflower butter.

These are particularly good served warm with coconut yogurt or ice cream.

caramel brownies

makes 12 brownies
prep time: 15 minutes
cook time: 25 minutes

½ cup ghee, plus extra
for greasing
⅔ cup finely chopped
dark chocolate
2 medium eggs
¾ cup coconut sugar
1 cup chickpea flour
⅛ cup cocoa powder
pinch of salt

½ cup dulce de leche
(page 45)

These brownies are soft with a slightly chewy centre and a
thick layer of dulce de leche swirled through. The sweetness
of the dulce de leche balances out the bitter notes of cocoa
perfectly.

Preheat the oven to 200°C/400°F/Gas 6 (180°C fan). Grease an
8-inch square baking pan and line with parchment paper.

In a small saucepan, melt the ghee over low heat. Add the
chopped chocolate, stirring until melted and well combined.
Remove from heat and set aside.

In a medium bowl, beat eggs and sugar with an electric whisk
for 10 minutes until thick. Add the chocolate-ghee mixture
and whisk until well combined.

Sift in the flour, cocoa powder and salt and gently fold until
just combined.

Pour ¾ of the brownie batter into the pan. Add spoonfuls of
the dulce de leche on top, making sure it's evenly spaced. Top
with the remaining brownie batter. Use a knife and swirl it
through the brownie batter to create a marbled effect.

Bake for 20-25 minutes until a metal skewer comes out clean.
Leave the brownies in the pan to cool completely before
slicing into squares.

Store in an airtight container in the fridge for 3-4 days.

notes
If you don't have dulce de leche, you can use a store-bought
caramel sauce. Alternatively, make your own date caramel:
blend ½ cup date spread (page 33) with 2 tablespoons milk.

cakes

cinnamon bun muffins

makes 14 muffins
prep time: 15 minutes
cook time: 15 minutes

cinnamon mix
¼ cup cinnamon
¼ cup coconut sugar
¼ cup melted ghee
2 tbsp boiling water

muffins
⅔ cup ghee, plus extra
for greasing
⅔ cup light honey
1 tsp vanilla extract
4 medium eggs
2½ cups oat flour
2 tsp baking powder
2 tsp baking soda

glaze
6 tbsp coconut butter

If you love cinnamon buns but don't love the time and effort that goes into making them, these are the perfect solution - fluffy cake meets cinnamon roll.

Preheat the oven to 200°C/400°F/Gas 6 (180°C fan). Grease a standard-size 12-cup muffin pan and line with parchment paper.

Combine the ingredients for the 'cinnamon mix' in a small bowl and set aside.

In a separate bowl, cream together the ghee and honey with an electric whisk until lightened in colour. Add the vanilla then the eggs one at a time, beating well after each addition. Whisk for 2-3 minutes. Sift in the oat flour, baking powder and baking soda, and fold with a rubber spatula until well combined. Use a cookie scoop or spoon to distribute the batter evenly between the muffin cups.

Drizzle about ½ teaspoon of the cinnamon mix on each muffin and swirl it around with a knife or a metal skewer.

Place on the middle rack of the oven and bake for 12-15 minutes.

To make the glaze, fill a saucepan with 2 inches of water and bring to a simmer. Place a heat-proof bowl over a saucepan, making sure it fits snugly. Add the coconut butter to the bowl and stir over medium-low heat until melted. Remove from the heat and set aside to cool.

Take the muffins out the oven and let them cool for 5 minutes. Remove from the pan and place on a cooling rack to cool completely. Finish with a drizzle of glaze on each muffin.

Store in an airtight container at room temperature for up to 5 days.

ube cream cake

makes 16 squares
prep time: 15 minutes
cook time: 20 minutes

I am happiest when I work with ingredients that are naturally vibrant in colour - ube is one of them. These little squares have a perfectly moist and fluffy sponge with a gorgeous layer of purple coconut cream in the middle.

cake
3 tbsp ghee, plus extra
for greasing
⅔ cup almond flour
6 tbsp coconut flour
1 tsp baking powder
1 tsp baking soda
4 medium eggs
½ cup light honey
½ cup filtered water
1 tsp vanilla extract

ube cream
½ cup mashed ube
(page 29)
½ cup coconut cream
(page 31)
1½ tbsp light honey
1 tbsp lemon juice

Preheat the oven to 200°C/400°F/Gas 6 (180°C fan). Grease two 8-inch square baking pans and line with parchment paper.

Sift the flours, baking powder and baking soda in a large bowl and mix. Set aside.

In a separate bowl, whisk the eggs, ghee, honey, water and vanilla extract. Slowly add the liquid mixture to the dry ingredients and fold with a spatula until combined.

Pour into the pans and smooth over with an angled metal spatula. Place the pans in the middle rack of the oven and bake for 15-20 minutes or until golden on top. Leave the sponge in the pan to cool completely.

To make the sweet potato cream, add the ube, coconut cream, honey and lemon juice to a food processor and blend until smooth.

Spread the sweet potato cream on one sponge, place the other on top and slice into 12 squares.

Store in an airtight container in the fridge for up to 3 days.

notes
Substitute ube for purple or white sweet potato. You can also use orange sweet potato but note that it has a higher water content than the others so the cream may not be as thick.

Don't be alarmed if your sponge starts to turn slightly blue or green. That's from the pigment in the sweet potato reacting with the baking soda in the sponge, it's completely safe!

If you don't have two 8-inch pans, use the same pan to bake the cake batter for two rounds. Or use a larger baking pan and divide the sponge in two. You can also use two 9-inch round springform cake pans.

chocolate & tahini bread

makes 1 medium loaf
prep time: 15 minutes
bake time: 55 minutes

I love a secret ingredient. No one that tries this cake will ever guess that there's cauliflower in here. It's super soft and fluffy and if you like tahini, you'll love this. It's great for breakfast - served heated and topped with coconut yogurt and fresh fruit.

---

ghee or oil for greasing
¾ cup tahini
1 cup coconut sugar
2 medium eggs
1 tsp vanilla extract
5 tbsp filtered water
¾ cup riced cauliflower
½ cup oat flour
½ cup coconut flour
1 tsp baking soda
1 tsp baking powder
¼ tsp salt
⅓ cup chopped walnuts
⅓ cup chopped dark chocolate

Preheat oven to 180°C/350°F/Gas 4 (160°C fan). Grease a large loaf pan and line with parchment paper.

Whisk the tahini and coconut sugar until combined. Add the eggs and vanilla extract and whisk for 2-3 minutes. Add the water and whisk, then add the cauliflower and stir to combine. Sift in the flours, baking soda, baking powder, salt, walnuts and chocolate. Fold until just combined. The batter should be thick.

Pour the batter into the loaf pan and smooth over with an angled palette knife. Place the pan in the middle of the oven and bake for 45-55 minutes. Allow the cake to sit in the pan for 10 minutes, then transfer to a cooling rack to cool completely before slicing.

Store in an airtight container at room temperature for 4-5 days.

notes
For riced cauliflower, place cauliflower florets in a food processor and pulse until rice-like. Alternatively use the bigger holes of a box grater to grate the florets.

basbousa

makes 24 mini squares
prep time: 15 minutes
bake time: 35 minutes

This Middle Eastern treat is infused with delicate flavours of honey and cardamom, which are similar to baklava. Except, instead of a pastry, basbousa takes the form of a cake soaked in a honey syrup and it's simpler to make. While this treat is typically made with semolina, I've used coconut and almond flour to make it gluten-free.

cake
¼ cup melted ghee,
plus extra for greasing
½ cup coconut flour
½ cup almond flour
½ tsp baking powder
¼ tsp ground cardamom
⅛ tsp salt
½ cup full-fat Greek yogurt
1 tsp vanilla extract
2 medium eggs

syrup
¾ cup water
½ cup light honey
1 pinch ground saffron

Preheat the oven to 200°C/400°F/Gas 6 (180°C fan). Grease an 8-inch square baking pan and line with parchment paper.

Sift the flours, baking powder, cardamom and salt in a large bowl, combine and set aside. In a separate bowl, whisk the ghee, yogurt, vanilla extract and eggs until well combined.

Slowly add the wet mixture to the dry ingredients and fold until combined.

Press the cake mix into the pan and smooth over with an angled palette knife. Use a sharp knife to carefully slice the cake mix into small diamonds or squares. Place the pan in the middle oven rack and bake for 30-35 minutes or until golden on top.

In the meantime, prepare the syrup. Add the water, honey and saffron to a medium saucepan over high heat. Bring to a boil for 5 minutes. Remove from the heat, add the lemon juice and set aside to cool.

Once the cake is ready, switch the oven off and remove the cake. Pour the cooled syrup over the warm cake, put it back in the oven, and leave to cool completely. Cut the cake again along the lines you cut earlier. Decorate with ground nuts and rose petals.

Store in an airtight container in the fridge for up to 5 days. Allow to reach room temperature before serving.

notes
I recommend allowing the cake to sit in the syrup for as long as possible before cutting. This gives the sponge time to absorb and hold onto the syrup better.

If you don't have ground saffron, use 3-4 threads of saffron instead.

Use an alternative yogurt instead of Greek yogurt to make it dairy-free.

cookies n cream cake

makes one 7-inch
double-layer cake
prep time: 1 hour, 30
minutes
bake time: 35 minutes

Cookies and cream cake is my all-time favourite. There was a time when I used to make this for almost every occasion (once you make it, you'll understand why). The cake is moist, fudgy and covered in fluffy whipped cream frosting and Noreo pieces.

---

cake
½ cup ghee, plus extra
for greasing
1½ cups oat flour
1¾ cups coconut sugar
⅔ cup cocoa powder
1 tsp espresso powder
1½ tsp baking powder
1½ tsp baking soda
2 medium eggs
2 tsp vanilla extract
2 cups boiling water

frosting
16 Noreos/Oreos
(page 61)
2½ cups heavy whipping
cream
5 tbsp maple syrup, or
to taste
1 tsp vanilla extract

Preheat the oven to 200°C/400°F/Gas 6 (180°C fan). Grease and line two 7-inch sandwich baking pans.

Place all the cake ingredients (except the boiling water) in a large mixing bowl. Stir lightly with a spatula, to avoid the flour going everywhere before using an electric whisk and beat the mixture while slowly adding the boiling water. Fold then whisk until smooth. It will be watery - don't worry, this is normal! Pour the batter into the pans and bake for 30–35 minutes, or until a metal skewer comes out clean. Leave the cakes to cool completely in the pans.

Place 10 Noreo (or Oreo) cookies in a plastic bag and hit them with a rolling pin until broken into chunky pieces. Set aside.

In a medium bowl, mix the cream, maple syrup and the vanilla extract with an electric whisk on medium-high speed until thickened with stiff peaks. Do not overmix. Add the crushed Noreos and stir to combine.

Once the cakes have cooled, run a sharp knife around the edge of the cake and carefully remove them from the pans. Place the first cake layer on a serving plate and spread a generous amount of frosting over the sponge (about ⅓). Place the second cake layer on top. Spread the rest of the frosting over and around the cake as smoothly as you can. Place in the fridge for 30 minutes to set.

Continue to the next page...

ganache
**¼ cup heavy whipping
cream**
**¼ cup finely chopped
dark chocolate**

To prepare the ganache, put the chopped dark chocolate in a bowl. Heat the cream in a small pan until steaming. Pour the cream over the chocolate and stir until the chocolate has melted. Allow the ganache to cool before using. It should be pourable but not too runny. Once cooled, use a dessert spoon to carefully drip the ganache down the sides of the cake, pour the rest on top of the cake and spread until smooth. Add the extra chopped Noreos on top to decorate.

Store in an airtight container in the fridge for 4-5 days.

notes

If you only have springform pans, you can use a large piece of parchment paper or foil to fully cover the base and sides of the pan, making sure that the batter is unable to seep its way out.

For a dairy-free cake, substitute the heavy whipping cream for whipped coconut cream.

You can also replace the maple syrup in the frosting with powdered sugar.

simple sponge cake

makes one 8-inch
round cake
prep time: 15 minutes
bake time: 30 minutes

¼ cup ghee, plus extra
for greasing
2 oranges, sliced
½ cup coconut flour
1 cup oat flour
½ tsp baking powder
½ tsp baking soda
pinch of salt
2 medium eggs
¾ cup light honey
1 tsp vanilla extract

This is the perfect last-minute cake for when you have guests over or if you want to make a quick cake as a gift. Double the recipe and combine it with your favourite frosting to turn it into a layered cake.

Preheat the oven to 200°C/400°F/Gas 6 (180°C fan).

Grease an 8-inch round springform cake pan. Arrange the orange slices on the base and set aside.

In a large mixing bowl, sift the flours, baking powder, baking soda and salt, mix and set aside.

In a separate bowl, whisk the eggs until foamy. Add the ghee, honey and vanilla extract and whisk for 2 minutes.

Add the egg mixture to the dry ingredients and fold with a rubber spatula until well combined.

Pour the batter into the pan and spread until smooth. Place the pan on the middle rack of the oven and bake for 25-30 minutes or until a metal skewer comes out clean.

Store in an airtight container at room temperature for 4-5 days.

notes

You can use any other sliced fruit for the base - figs, peaches, strawberries etc.

lemon crumb cake

makes a medium loaf
prep time: 10 minutes
bake time: 1 hour

This lemon cake loaf is zesty and refreshing. The berries add a gorgeous burst of colour and the streusel gives a little crunch on top. Perfect for an afternoon tea.

---

crumb topping
¼ cup oat flour
1 tsp honey
1 tsp ghee
zest of ½ a lemon

cake
¼ cup ghee, plus extra
for greasing
½ cup almond flour
½ cup oat flour
½ cup coconut flour
1 tsp baking soda
¼ tsp salt
¼ cup light honey
3 medium eggs
zest of 1 lemon
2 tbsp lemon juice
2 handfuls of mixed
berries

Preheat the oven to 180°C/350°F/Gas 4 (160°C fan). Grease and line a medium loaf pan.

Using your fingers, combine the ingredients for the crumb topping in a small bowl until they clump together.

Sift the almond flour, oat flour, coconut flour, baking soda and salt in a large mixing bowl. Mix and set aside.

In a medium bowl, whisk together the ghee and honey with an electric whisk until it lightens in colour. Add each egg, one at a time, whisking after each addition. Add the lemon juice and zest and whisk until well combined.

Slowly pour the wet mixture into the dry ingredients while folding with a rubber spatula. Fold in the berries and pour into the loaf pan.

Sprinkle the crumb topping on top. Place the pan on the middle rack of the oven to and bake for 55-65 minutes or until a metal skewer comes out clean.

Take the loaf out of the oven and allow to rest in the pan for 10 minutes. Turn out on a cooling rack to cool completely.

Store in an airtight container in the fridge for 4-5 days.

notes
To make it grain-free, substitute the oat flour for almond flour.

carrot cake squares

makes 16 squares
prep time: 35 minutes
bake time: 25 minutes

cake
3 tbsp ghee, plus extra
for greasing
2 large eggs, separated
3 tbsp water
⅓ cup almond flour
⅔ cup oat flour
½ tsp baking powder
½ tsp baking soda
1 tbsp cinnamon
1 cup grated carrots
½ cup chopped walnuts
½ cup coconut sugar

frosting
¼ cup coconut yogurt
¼ cup cream cheese
1 tbsp maple syrup

nuts to decorate

What's not to love about carrot cake? It's moist and fluffy with a subtle hint of spice, topped with a silky-smooth cream cheese frosting. This is not one to miss.

Preheat the oven to 200°C/400°F/Gas 6 (180°C fan). Grease an 8-inch square baking pan and line with parchment paper.

In a large mixing bowl, whisk the egg yolks, ghee and water until combined. Sift in the flours, baking powder, baking soda, cinnamon, carrots and walnuts and set aside.

In a clean, dry bowl, add the egg whites and whisk with an electric whisk on high until white and fluffy. Gradually add the coconut sugar while whisking until soft peaks form. Add ⅓ of the egg whites to the egg yolk mixture and fold until combined. Add the remaining egg whites and fold until just combined.

Pour the batter into the prepared pan and bake for 20-25 minutes or until a metal skewer comes out clean. Leave to cool completely before frosting.

For the frosting, whisk together the coconut yogurt, cream cheese and maple syrup in a medium bowl. Spread the frosting over the cake and finish with a sprinkle of nuts.

Store in an airtight container in the fridge for 4-5 days.

notes
For a layered cake, double up the recipe and bake in two 8-inch round cake pans.

pistachio cake

makes a medium loaf
prep time: 12 minutes
cook time: 1 hour

Pistachio is one of those family-favourite flavours, especially in a dessert. This cake is perfectly moist and the flavours paired with honey and vanilla, really sing.

---

cake
⅓ cup ghee, plus extra
for greasing
1 cup pistachios,
shelled, extra for
decoration
1 tsp baking powder
1 tsp baking soda
¾ cup oat flour
½ cup coconut flour
¾ cup light honey
1 tsp vanilla extract
4 medium eggs
⅓ cup milk of choice

topping (optional)
1 cup coconut yogurt
1 cup figs, chopped

Preheat the oven to 200°C/400°F/Gas 6 (180°C fan). Grease a medium loaf pan and line with parchment paper.

Put the pistachios in a food processor and blitz until it's a fine powder.

Sift the baking powder, baking soda, oat flour, coconut flour and wheatgrass in a large bowl. Add the ground pistachios, combine and set aside.

In a separate bowl, whisk the honey, ghee and vanilla extract. Add the eggs one at a time, whisking after each addition. Add the milk and mix until well combined. Make sure you use a spatula to scrape the honey that might be stuck at the base of the bowl.

Gradually add the honey mixture to the dry ingredients, folding with a spatula until combined.

Pour into the prepared loaf pan and bake for 50-60 minutes or until a metal skewer comes out clean.

Leave the cake to cool in the pan for 30 minutes, then remove and transfer to a cooling rack to cool completely. Spread the coconut yogurt on top and decorate with figs and pistachios.

Store in an airtight container in the fridge for up to 5 days.

notes
Raw pistachios are used in this cake, but roasted can also be used.

misc

peach & berry crumble

makes one 8-inch
crumble
prep time: 5 minutes
bake time: 35 minutes

Crumble isn't usually a dessert I tend to go for, but when it's in front of me, I just want to finish the whole thing! This crumble is fun to put together and it's easy to make it your own. You can use different fruits or spices, depending on what you fancy and what's in season.

ghee or oil for greasing

filling
3 cups sliced peaches
1 cup blackberries
2 tbsp lemon juice
1 lemon zest
3 tbsp coconut sugar
1 tbsp tapioca flour
½ tsp cinnamon
pinch of salt

crumble
1 cup oat flour
1 cup almond flour
¼ cup coconut sugar
3 tbsp coconut oil

Preheat the oven to 180°C/350°F/Gas 4 (160°C fan). Lightly grease an 8-inch pie dish.

In a large mixing bowl, mix all the filling ingredients. Pour into the pie dish and set aside.

To make the crumble, add the oat flour, almond flour, coconut sugar and coconut oil to a medium bowl. Use your fingers to rub the ingredients together until they clump together and resemble small crumbs.

Sprinkle the crumble evenly over the fruit filling in the pie dish.

Place the pie dish in the middle of the oven and bake for 30-35 minutes or until golden on top. Allow the crumble to rest for 5 minutes before serving with warm custard (page 39), whipped cream or ice cream.

Store in an airtight container in the fridge for 3-4 days.

notes
To make it nut-free, use 2 cups oat flour. Alternatively, to make it grain-free/ paleo, use 2 cups almond flour.

(V) (DF)

cinnamon rolls

makes 6 rolls
prep time: 15 minutes
cook time: 25 minutes
setting time: 1 hour 15 minutes

rolls
1¼ cup oat flour, divided
1¼ cup tapioca flour, divided
¾ tsp instant yeast
½ cup warm water
1 medium egg, room temperature
2 tbsp light honey
3 tbsp ghee

filling
3 tbsp ghee, plus extra for greasing
1 tbsp cinnamon
½ cup coconut sugar

egg wash
1 medium egg
1 tbsp milk

The perfect cosy treat on a cold winter's day... or any given day, let's be honest. Cinnamon rolls can take a little while to make, but I can confidently tell you that these babies are worth it!

In a large mixing bowl, add ¾ cup oat flour, ¾ cup tapioca flour, yeast, water, egg, honey and ghee. Mix until well combined. It will have the consistency of a thick paste. Cover the bowl with cling film and let it sit in a warm place for 40 minutes to 1 hour or until doubled in size.

Add the remaining ½ cup tapioca and ½ cup oat flour to the paste and knead until a dough forms.

On a large piece of parchment paper, sprinkle some flour and use a rolling pin to roll out the dough to roughly a 12x9-inch rectangle.

For the filling, spread the ghee over the dough, leaving a ¼ -inch gap from the edges.

Mix the cinnamon and coconut sugar in a bowl. Sprinkle the cinnamon mixture over the dough and gently rub it into the ghee. Use the parchment paper to help you tightly roll up the dough from the 12-inch edge, then seal the edges. Using a sharp serrated knife, cut off each end of the dough to neaten up. Slice into 6 even rolls.

Continue to the next page ...

frosting
2 tbsp cream cheese
2 tbsp coconut cream
(page 31)
½ tbsp maple syrup
½ tsp vanilla extract

Lightly grease a round 9-inch dish or equivalent and place the rolls inside. Cover the dish with cling film and let the rolls rest in a warm place for 30-35 minutes until they have risen.

Preheat the oven to 200°C/400°F/Gas 6 (180°C fan).

For the egg wash, whisk the egg and milk in a small bowl and use a pastry brush to brush the tops of the rolls. Place in the middle rack of the oven to bake for 20-25 minutes until golden.

Make the frosting by whisking the ingredients together in a small bowl until combined. Once the buns are out the oven, allow them to rest for 10 minutes before spreading the icing on top.

Store in an airtight container in the fridge for up to 4 days.

rhubarb galette

makes 1 galette
prep time: 15 minutes
cook time: 40 minutes

A gorgeous and rustic summer dessert. It's like a pie, but with less effort. You don't need to spend your time fiddling around with the base and topping. Just wrap the pastry around the filling without the stress of making it look pretty. Yet, it's just as satisfying to eat and equally as impressive!

filling
½ cup coconut sugar
½ tsp cinnamon
1 tbsp tapioca flour
1 tsp vanilla extract
2 tbsp lemon juice
1 lemon zest
pinch of nutmeg
400g /14oz trimmed rhubarb

crust
1 cup oat flour
½ cup tapioca flour
1 large egg
2 tbsp ghee, room temperature
2½ tbsp water
1 tsp vanilla extract
pinch of salt
1 tbsp coconut sugar

egg wash
1 medium egg
1 tsp water

Preheat the oven to 200°C/400°F/Gas 6 (180°C fan).

In a small bowl, add the coconut sugar, cinnamon, tapioca flour, vanilla extract, lemon juice, zest and nutmeg. Stir to combine and set aside.

For the crust, add all the ingredients to a large mixing bowl. Mix until it turns into a dough.

Dust a little flour on parchment paper and roll out the dough into a circle with a diameter of roughly 11 inches.

Transfer to a large baking tray to assemble. Using a pastry brush, brush the dough with the sugar filling, leaving a 1-inch gap from the edges. Cut the rhubarb into sticks to fit into the centre and arrange them side by side into a circle, leaving a 1½ inch gap from the edge then brush the tops with the sugar filling. Fold over the edges of the crust towards the centre and pour the rest of the sugar filling inside.

In a small bowl, whisk the egg and water. Use a pastry brush to lightly coat the crust with the egg wash and sprinkle a little coconut sugar on top.

Place the tray in the middle of the oven and bake for 35-40 minutes or until the edges are golden and crisp. Allow to rest for 10 minutes before slicing and serving. Store in an airtight container in the fridge for up to 4 days.

notes
This galette can be made with any other pie-filling fruit.

caramel skillet cookie

makes 1 giant cookie
prep time: 10 minutes
cook time: 25 minutes

This is what I'd order for dessert without hesitation. It has everything I look for and more. Warm, gooey chocolate chip cookie base, dulce de leche and a golden crust. Topped with vanilla bean ice cream that slowly melts in.

---

cookie
⅓ cup softened ghee, plus extra for greasing
½ cup mashed Japanese sweet potato (page 29)
2 medium eggs
½ cup coconut sugar
1 tsp vanilla extract
½ cup coconut flour
½ cup almond flour
1 tsp baking soda
½ cup chopped dark chocolate
⅓ cup chilled dulce de leche (page 45)

caramel sauce
⅓ cup dulce de leche
½ tsp tapioca flour
½ cup water

Preheat the oven to 200°C/400°F/Gas 6 (180°C fan). Grease a 9-inch ovenproof frying pan. In a large mixing bowl, add the sweet potato, eggs, ghee, coconut sugar and vanilla extract and whisk until well combined. Sift in the flours and baking soda and stir to combine. Fold in the chopped dark chocolate with a rubber spatula.

Press ⅓ of the cookie dough into the pan and spread ⅓ cup dulce de leche on top. Carefully add the rest of the cookie dough and flatten.

Place the pan in the middle of the oven and bake for 20-25 minutes or until golden on top.

To make the caramel sauce, add the dulce de leche and tapioca flour to a small saucepan and whisk on medium-high heat. Add the water and whisk. Allow the sauce to bubble while whisking every so often for about 10 minutes, until thick and drizzly.

Once the cookie is ready, let it rest for 5 minutes before serving. Top with vanilla ice cream, cream or coconut yogurt and drizzle the caramel sauce on top.

Store in an airtight container in the fridge for 4-5 days.

   (P) (DF) (NF) (GF)

notes

If you don't have dulce the leche, you can skip the caramel sauce and add an extra ¼ cup coconut sugar to the cookie.

Alternatively, you might prefer to use store-bought caramel or another sweet spread like date spread (page 33) or halva spread (page 41) to fill and top the cookie.

peanut butter & jelly cups

makes 8 cups
prep time: 15 minutes
cook time: 10 minutes
set time: 40 minutes

crust
¼ cup roasted peanut butter
2 tbsp coconut sugar
½ tsp vanilla extract
¼ cup oat flour
⅛ tsp of salt

filling
½ cup strawberry chia jam (page 43)

topping
⅔ cup finely chopped dark chocolate
freeze-dried berries

The classic duo topped with a thick layer of dark chocolate makes the most perfect little snack. It has a crumbly, salty peanut crust balanced with a sweet jam filling. They freeze well, which makes them a convenient treat so next time you feel like it's peanut-butter-and-jelly time, just grab a cup from the freezer and enjoy!

Preheat the oven to 200°C/400°F/Gas 6 (180°C fan). Line a standard size 12-cup muffin pan with cupcake liners.

In a large bowl, combine the peanut butter, coconut sugar, vanilla extract, oat flour and salt. Mix until a dough forms. Divide the dough into 8 pieces. Roll into balls and flatten in your palms. Press each round piece into the base of the cupcake liner and slightly up the sides.

Bake the crust for 10 minutes or until it starts to turn golden.

Once cooled completely, add one tablespoon of jam inside each crust. Place in the freezer to set for at least 20 minutes.

Fill a saucepan with 2 inches of water and bring to a simmer. Place a heat-proof bowl over the saucepan, making sure it fits snugly. Add the chopped chocolate and stir over medium heat until melted. Remove from the heat.

Spoon the melted chocolate over the frozen cups and spread evenly. Sprinkle with freeze-dried berries to decorate.

Store in an airtight container in the fridge for up to 4 days or freeze for up to 3 months. Allow to reach room temperature before serving.

notes
Use unsweetened peanut butter without additives. If your peanut butter is salted, don't add the extra salt for the crust.
You can substitute strawberry chia jam for your jam of choice.
To make it grain-free, substitute oat flour for almond flour.

cookies n cream cheesecake

makes one 8-inch cheesecake
prep time: 20 minutes
cook time: 1 hour, 10 minutes
chill time: 9 hours

She's beauty and she's grace, she's a cheeseless cheesecake. We've got a crumbly Noreo crust, a creamy filling with Noreo pieces, topped with even more Noreos and finally a drizzle of chocolate fudge sauce. Whether you're an Oreo or *Noreo* lover, you will love this recipe!

---

crust
¼ cup ghee, plus extra for greasing
16 Noreos (page 61)

filling
1 cup cannellini beans, cooked
⅔ cup maple syrup
1 tsp vanilla extract
1 tbsp lemon juice
½ cup nutritional yeast
⅛ tsp salt
1½ cup coconut yogurt
3 large eggs
10 chopped Noreos

Preheat the oven to 200°C/400°F/Gas 6 (180°C fan). Grease an 8-inch springform pan and set aside.

For the crust, add the Noreos to the food processor and blend until fine, add the melted ghee until the crumbs stick together. Press the crust in the pan along the base and a little up the sides. Use the back of a spoon to smooth down. Bake for 10 minutes then remove from the oven and set aside.

Reduce the oven temperature to 170°C/325°F/ Gas 3 (150°C fan). Place a medium rectangular pan on the bottom rack of your oven and fill halfway with boiling water.

Clean and dry the food processor. Add the cannellini beans, maple syrup, vanilla extract, lemon juice, nutritional yeast, and salt and blend until smooth. Add the coconut yogurt and pulse until combined. Scrape down the sides and add the eggs one at a time, pulsing in between until incorporated. Fold in the chopped Noreos then pour over the crust in the springform pan.

Continue to the next page...

chocolate fudge sauce
1 tbsp coconut oil
¼ cup cocoa powder
2 tbsp maple syrup
1-2 tbsp water

10 chopped Noreos for topping

Bake for 1 hour or until the centre of the cheesecake is only slightly jiggly and golden on top.

Once the cheesecake is done and the oven is off, open the oven door and place a wooden spoon in between the door and the oven to keep it slightly ajar. Leave the cheesecake to cool inside for an hour, then take it out to cool completely.
Once cooled, transfer to the fridge to set for 8 hours.

To make the chocolate fudge sauce, melt the coconut oil in a small saucepan on low heat. Once melted, remove from heat and add the rest of the ingredients and whisk until combined.

Run a sharp knife around the cake and remove from the pan.

Arrange the Noreos on the cake and drizzle the chocolate fudge sauce on top.

Store in an airtight container in the fridge for 4-5 days.

notes

The coconut yogurt can be replaced with coconut cream. I recommend adding an extra tablespoon of lemon juice for tanginess.

saffron lava cakes

makes 4 puddings
prep time: 15 minutes
cook time: 12 minutes

There's nothing more satisfying than cutting into a cake to
a steaming molten middle - talk about the finer things in life.
These luxurious little beauties are fragrant mini cakes with a
creamy saffron and white chocolate centre.

sponge
¼ cup ghee, plus extra
for greasing
6 tbsp oat flour
pinch of salt
⅛ tsp ground saffron
1½ tsp boiling water
45g/2.5oz chopped
white chocolate
2 tbsp maple syrup
½ tsp vanilla extract
2 large eggs
2 large egg yolks

Preheat the oven to 200°C/400°F/Gas 6 (180°C fan). Lightly grease
four pudding moulds or ramekins.

In a large bowl combine the oat flour and salt and set aside.

Place the saffron in a small saucepan with the boiling hot water.
Give it a swirl and let sit for a couple of minutes. Set the heat on
low, then add the white chocolate, maple syrup and ghee and
whisk until melted and combined. Take off the heat and set aside
to cool.

In a medium bowl, whisk the eggs and egg yolks. Slowly pour in
the white chocolate mixture to the eggs and fold until combined.

Pour the mixture into the bowl of flour and fold until just
combined. Divide the mixture between the pudding moulds.

Place in the middle of the oven and bake for 10-12 minutes or
until slightly golden on top.

Allow the puddings to rest at room temperature for 10 minutes,
then run a small sharp knife around the edges. Turn onto a plate
and serve with coconut yogurt, cream or ice cream.

notes

Serve and enjoy while warm and fresh. This dessert doesn't keep
well when stored the next day, as the centre will harden.

If you don't have pudding moulds or ramekins, use the moulds of
a muffin pan, this may yield more puddings and they'll need less
time in the oven, so keep an eye on them.

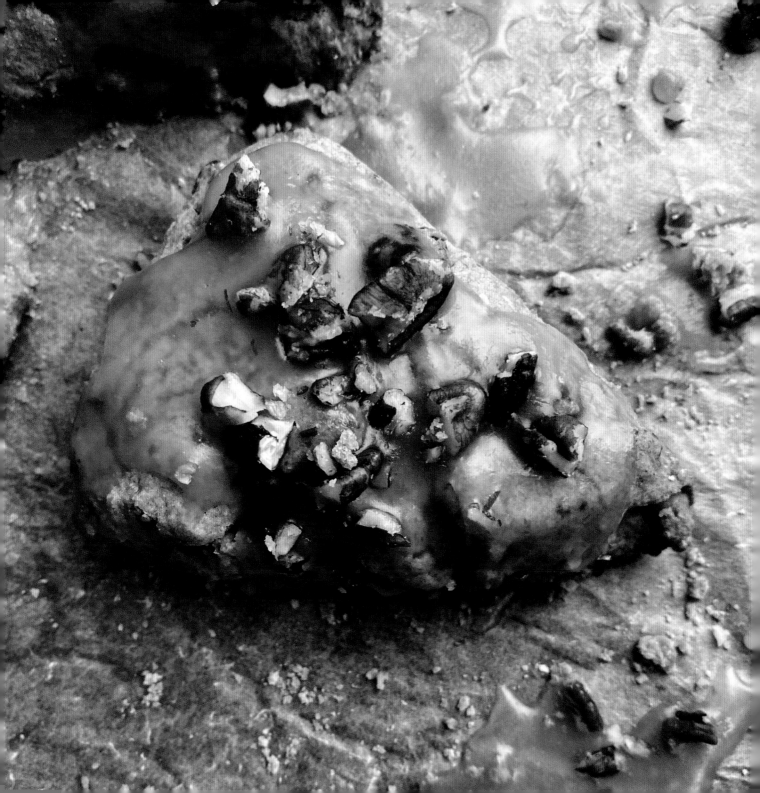

maple butter scones

makes 8 scones
prep time: 12 minutes
cook time: 25 minutes

Maple syrup and pecans in baked goods make me feel some type of way. It's got that cosy combination that makes you want to curl by the fireplace with a movie or a good book and a hot cup of tea. These tender and crumbly scones are best served warm, with a drizzle of maple glaze.

scones
1 ½ cups oat flour
2 tbsp tapioca flour
1 tsp baking powder
½ tsp salt
¼ cup cold cubed butter
¼ cup maple syrup
1 medium egg, whisked
½ cup chopped pecans
milk, to brush

maple glaze
¼ cup coconut butter
3 tbsp maple syrup
1 tbsp milk
pinch of salt

Preheat the oven to 200°C/400°F/Gas 6 (180°C fan) and line a baking tray with parchment paper.

Combine the flours, baking powder and salt in a large mixing bowl. Add the butter to the flours and use your fingers to rub the ingredients together until it starts to resemble small crumbs. Add the maple syrup, egg, water and pecans and mix with your hands until a dough forms. Shape into a ball and press the top to flatten into a wheel, then slice into eight wedges. Transfer the scones to the baking tray and use a pastry brush to brush the tops with milk.

Bake for 20-25 minutes or until lightly golden on top.

For the maple glaze, add the coconut butter to a small saucepan on low heat until melted. Remove from the heat then add the maple syrup, milk and salt and mix until combined. The consistency should be thick and drizzly. It will firm up the more it cools.

Leave the scones in the tray to cool for 15 minutes then drizzle with the maple glaze and serve.

Store in an airtight container in the fridge for up to 5 days.

self-saucing sticky toffee pudding

makes one pudding
prep time: 20 minutes
cook time: 35 minutes

This pudding is something else - one batter that makes both a cake and a sticky bubbling toffee sauce, all by itself. Once you bring this out of the oven, you'll feel proud that you just created this beautiful baby. It's without a doubt best served warm, preferably with custard.

sponge
⅓ cup coconut oil, melted, plus extra for greasing
⅔ cup packed pitted dates
2 cups oat flour
¼ cup coconut sugar
2 tsp baking powder
¼ tsp salt
2 tsp vanilla extract
1 cup milk

sauce
½ cup coconut sugar
2 cups boiling water

Cover the pitted dates with warm water and leave to soak for 1 hour.

Preheat oven to 190°C/370°F/Gas 5 (170°C fan). Grease a 9-inch baking dish.

Drain the dates and place them on a chopping board. Finely chop, then set aside.

In a large mixing bowl, combine the oat flour, coconut sugar, baking powder and salt then set aside.

In another bowl, whisk the coconut oil, vanilla extract and milk until smooth. Slowly pour the milk mixture into the flour mixture and fold. Add the dates and fold until evenly distributed.

Pour the mixture into the baking dish and use an angled palette knife to smooth it over.

Sprinkle ½ cup of coconut sugar over the batter and then pour the boiling water over the top - do not mix, just let it sit on top of the batter.

Bake for 35-40 minutes, until the centre is set and the sauce is bubbling. Remove from the oven and leave to cool for 10 minutes.
Serve with warm custard (page 39), your favourite ice cream or yogurt.

Store in an airtight container in the fridge for up to 4 days.

notes

I recommend Medjool dates for their flavour and texture, however, any other date will work.

This is best eaten fresh out of the oven. It's still good once stored, but the sponge will absorb the sauce so it will have a different quality.

no bake

cookie dough nice cream

makes 1 small loaf pan
prep time: 15 minutes
chill time: 6 hours

That's right, we have got ourselves nice cream with cookie dough and chocolate chunks swirled throughout. All made with the not-so-humble sweet potato. Yes, we have come a long way to get here and there's no turning back.

¾ cup cashews
½ cup cookie dough
(page 35)
¾ cup mashed
Japanese sweet
potato (page 29)
¾ cup coconut
cream (page 31)
¼ cup maple syrup,
or to taste
1 tsp vanilla extract
pinch of salt
½ cup chopped dark
chocolate

Soak the cashews overnight in a bowl of water. If you are short on time, soak them in boiling hot water for an hour.

Line a small loaf pan or a container with a lid and parchment paper then set aside.

Wet your hands with a little water before handling the cookie dough to prevent sticking. Separate into small 1-inch pieces, roll into balls and set aside.

Drain the cashews. Place the cashews, sweet potato, coconut cream, maple syrup, vanilla extract and salt into a food processor or high-speed blender and blend at high speed until smooth. Make sure to take intervals to scrape down the sides with a rubber spatula.

Stir in the cookie dough balls and chopped chocolate and pour into the loaf pan or container and cover with parchment paper or cling film.

Transfer to the freezer to set for 6 hours. When you're ready to serve, leave the nice cream out at room temperature for 10 minutes.

---

notes

If the cookie dough is too sticky to handle, add a little extra oat flour and mix until it becomes drier.

If you don't want to add cookie dough and chocolate chunks, you can try incorporating other additions such as Noreos (page 61), fruit pieces or a swirl of dulce de leche (page 45).

chocolate & pistachio stuffed dates

makes 10 stuffed dates
prep time: 10 minutes
chill time: 10 minutes

These are hands down the most simple type of treat to put together and enjoy. I love this variation - when you bite into it, you get the crunch from the chocolate and pistachio, the creamy centre, and the chewiness from the dates.

---

10 medjool dates
¼ cup coconut yogurt
¼ tsp ground cardamom
75 g dark chocolate
2 tbsp pistachio kernals

rose petals to decorate

Slice the dates lengthwise down the centre and take out the pit and open up the dates to create space for the fillings.

Fill a saucepan with water and bring to a simmer. Place a heat-proof bowl over the saucepan, making sure it fits snugly. Place the chopped chocolate in the bowl and stir until melted. Take off heat.

Use a fork and dip a date in the melted chocolate until covered. Let the excess drip off before placing on a wire rack. Repeat until all the dates are covered in chocolate. Transfer to the freezer to set for 5-10 minutes or until the chocolate has hardened.

In the meantime, mix coconut yogurt with ground cardamom in a small bowl. Fill the chocolate covered dates with about a teaspoon of coconut yogurt.

Roughly chop the pistachios and stuff them inside the dates. Finally sprinkle with rose petals to decorate.

Store in an airtight container in the fridge for up to 1 week.

notes

If you're short on time you can stuff the dates with chocolate pieces rather than coating in melted chocolate.

This is one of those recipes that is easy to get creative with - you can try it out with different nut butter, cream cheese, halva spread (page 41) or even cookie dough (page 35).

mint choc chunk bars

makes 12 bars
prep time: 12 minutes
chill time: 8 hours

filling
1 cup cashews
¼ cup maple syrup
1 cup coconut cream
(page 31)
4-5 drops peppermint
essential oil
¼ tsp spirulina
½ cup chopped dark
chocolate, plus extra
to decorate

crust
1 cup oat flour
¼ cup dates, pitted
¼ cup cocoa powder
¼ cup cacao nibs
⅓ cup water

Mint chocolate chip is one of my all-time favourite ice cream flavours - I like the balance between the creamy texture and refreshing mint flavour. These bars are like an open-faced ice cream sandwich with a crumbly cocoa crust.

Soak the cashews overnight in a bowl of water. If you are short on time, soak them in boiling water for an hour.

Line an 8-inch square baking pan with parchment paper and set aside.

Place all the crust ingredients, except for the water, into a food processor and blend. Scrape down the sides and blend while adding water, 1 tablespoon at a time, until it turns into a dough.

Press the crust evenly into the base of the tray and set aside.

Clean and dry the food processor. Place the ingredients for the filling except for the chocolate chunks. Blend until smooth, taking intervals to scrape down the sides. Stir in ½ cup of chopped chocolate then pour the mixture into the pan. Sprinkle the rest of the chocolate on top and put in the freezer to set for 8 hours.

Slice into 12 bars and store in an airtight container in the freezer for up to 3 months.

notes
You may need to adjust the amount of water for the crust depending on how moist your dates are. Add the water gradually until it forms a dough.

The spirulina is for colour. You can also use chlorella or wheatgrass powder, or skip out on the powders altogether.

If you don't have cacao nibs, substitute them for chopped dark chocolate.

jam nonuts

makes 16 balls
prep time: 20 minutes
chill time: 1 hour

Inspired by the jam doughnut. But, this ain't no doughnut, they're Nonuts and they turned out to be a popular favourite amongst my family and friends. The balls have a malted-milk-like flavour and cake batter consistency. The jam filling in the middle is just that cherry on top.

filling
8 tsp strawberry
chia jam (page 43)

balls
1 cup oat flour
½ cup tapioca flour
2 tbsp ghee
¼ cup maple syrup
1 tsp vanilla extract

Line a baking tray with parchment paper and put 16 small drops (about half a teaspoon) of chia jam. Put in the freezer for at least an hour to firm up.

In a large mixing bowl, add the oat flour, tapioca flour, vanilla extract, ghee and maple syrup and mix until combined. The texture should be like cookie dough.

Take a palmful of the dough, roll into a ball roughly the size of a golf ball and flatten like a pancake. Add a ball of frozen jam in the centre and carefully wrap the dough around the jam to seal the edges and roll into a ball. If the jam starts to melt, pop the tray back in the freezer to firm up and continue.

Roll the balls in tapioca flour and place on a plate.

Store in an airtight container, in the fridge for up to 4 days.

notes

If you find the dough to be too crumbly (i.e. it starts to form cracks), add a little water and mix until it's more pliable.

Feel free to get creative with other fillings like dulce de leche, halva spread, nut butter, etc.

caramel cups

makes 6 caramel cups
prep time: 35 minutes
chill time: 20 minutes

These do not disappoint; by now you know that I'm a fan of chocolate and caramel - this is a variation that your tastebuds will thank you for. The cups start with an oat crust, filled with fudgy caramel then topped with a thick layer of chocolate.

---

crust
¼ cup coconut oil, melted, plus extra for greasing
¼ cup date spread (page 33)
1½ cups oat flour
¼ tsp salt

filling
½ cup almond butter
¼ cup date spread
2 tbsp maple syrup
2 tbsp milk
¼ tsp salt

65 g dark chocolate

Lightly grease a silicone standard-size muffin mould and set aside.

For the crust, add the coconut oil, date spread and oat flour in a large mixing bowl and combine with your fingers until it resembles a crumbly dough.

Divide the dough between 6 cups and press down firmly to cover the base and a little up the sides and set aside.

For the caramel, whisk the almond butter, date spread, maple syrup and salt until combined. Slowly add the milk and whisk until smooth and drizzly.

Spoon the caramel into each crust, dividing evenly between the cups. Place in the fridge to set while you prepare the chocolate.

Fill a saucepan with water and bring to a simmer. Place a heat-proof bowl over the saucepan, making sure it fits snugly. Place the chopped chocolate in the bowl and stir until melted.

Spoon the dark chocolate over each cup and spread evenly with the back of a spoon. Place in the fridge to set for 15-20 minutes. Once the chocolate has completely set, remove the cups from the mould and serve.

Store in an airtight container in the fridge for up to 1 week, or freeze for up to 1 month.

notes

These cups would also work well filled with any nut butter, dulce de leche (page 45) or strawberry chia jam (page 43).

If you don't have a silicone muffin mould, use a regular muffin pan and line with cupcake cases.

If your dates aren't soft, soak them in a bowl of hot water for an hour.

To make these grain-free, replace oat flour with almond flour.

hazelnut creme bites

makes 25 bites
prep time: 40 minutes
chill time: 6 hours,
10 minutes

filling
¼ cup cocoa butter
½ cup coconut cream
(page 31)
½ cup hazelnut butter
¼ cup maple syrup
2 tsp maca powder
1 tsp vanilla extract

1 cup finely chopped
dark chocolate

Kinder Bueno is without a doubt, one of the best chocolates out there and these little bites are inspired by them. They are coated in dark chocolate and filled with smooth hazelnut cream.

Line a 6-inch square pan with parchment paper and set aside.

Place a heat-proof bowl over the saucepan, making sure it fits snugly. Place the chopped chocolate in the bowl and stir until melted. Safely remove the bowl from the saucepan and set aside to cool.

Place the coconut cream, hazelnut butter, melted cocoa butter, maple syrup, maca powder and vanilla extract in a blender and blend until smooth. Pour into the pan and put in the freezer to set for 6 hours.

Take the frozen filling out of the parchment paper and place it on a chopping board. With a sharp knife, carefully slice into 1-inch cubes, then put back in the freezer while you melt the chocolate.

Fill a saucepan with water and bring to a simmer. Place a heat-proof bowl over the saucepan, making sure it fits snugly. Place the chopped chocolate in the bowl and stir until melted. Take off heat.

Drop a frozen hazelnut cube in the melted chocolate, use a fork to rotate the cube until covered, then transfer onto a wire rack to set. Repeat this step until all pieces are coated in chocolate. Drizzle any excess chocolate on top, then place in the fridge to set for 10 minutes.

Store in an airtight container in the fridge for up to 4 days, or the freezer for up to 1 month. If frozen, allow the bites to thaw for 30 minutes before serving.

notes
Cocoa butter can be subbed for coconut butter.
Maca adds a subtle caramel, malt-like taste, but it can be left out. If you find that the melted chocolate is starting to harden after dipping the hazelnut cubes in it, place the bowl back on top of the saucepan on low heat, and add a little coconut oil to bring it back to a drizzly consistently.

141

white chocolate tahini squares

makes 16 squares
prep time: 15 minutes
chill time: 35 minutes

These gorgeous bars have a crumbly oat crust, with a layer of a sweet creamy tahini filling, coated with white chocolate. They're easy to assemble and even easier to devour!

---

crust
3 tbsp softened ghee, plus extra for greasing
1½ cups oat flour
2 tbsp maple syrup

tahini filling
1 cup tahini, plus extra to decorate
¼ cup maple syrup
2 tbsp coconut oil
1 tsp vanilla extract

white chocolate
¼ cup coconut butter
¼ cup cocoa butter
1 tsp maple syrup
½ tsp vanilla extract

sesame seeds & rose petals to decorate

Grease an 8-inch baking pan and line with parchment paper.

Place all the ingredients for the crust in a bowl and mix until it comes together to a dough. Press the crust into the base of the baking pan and set aside.

Whisk the ingredients for the tahini filling in a small saucepan over low heat until combined. Pour over the crust and spread evenly.

Place the tray in the freezer to set for at least 15 minutes.

In the meantime, fill a saucepan with water and bring to a simmer. Place a heat-proof bowl over the saucepan, making sure it fits snugly. Add the ingredients for the white chocolate and stir until it is mostly melted, safely remove the bowl from the heat and keep stirring until smooth and pour. Spread the white chocolate over the tahini filling, smooth over with an angled palette knife and set in the freezer for at least 20 minutes.

To decorate, you can drizzle tahini and sprinkle sesame seeds and rose petals. Use a sharp knife to slice the bar into 16 squares.

Store in an airtight container in the fridge for up to 1 week, or in the freezer for up to 1 month.

notes

If you're not a fan of tahini, swap it with any other nut butter.
To make it vegan-friendly, substitute the ghee for coconut oil.
To make it grain-free, substitute the oat flour for almond flour.

    (NF) (P) (DF) (GF) (V)

cookie dough bites

makes 16 bites
prep time: 15 minutes
chill time: 2 hours
20 minutes

base
1 cup cookie dough
(page 35)

filling
⅓ cup coconut yogurt
½ tsp vanilla extract

shell
1¼ cups finely
chopped dark
chocolate

Delicious little bites: rich cookie dough base accompanied by creamy coconut yogurt and coated with rich dark chocolate. They make a great snack or treat to have with a cup of tea.

Roll out a piece of parchment paper. With slightly wet hands, flatten the cookie dough onto the parchment paper and shape into roughly a 6x6-inch square.

Run a sharp knife under hot water to prevent sticking and slice the cookie dough into 16 little squares.

In a small bowl, combine the coconut yogurt with vanilla extract.

Spoon coconut yogurt on top of each square and spread to cover the base. Carefully transfer the parchment paper onto a baking pan and place in the freezer to set for at least 2 hours.

Fill a saucepan with water and bring to a simmer. Place a heat-proof bowl over the saucepan, making sure it fits snugly. Place the chopped chocolate in the bowl and stir until melted. Take off the heat.

Using two forks, gently dip each frozen piece into the melted chocolate and transfer onto a wire rack. Transfer to the fridge to set for 20 minutes.

Store in an airtight container in the fridge for up to a week or in the freezer for up to 3 months.

notes

If freezing, allow to thaw for 30 minutes before serving.

If you find that the melted chocolate is starting to harden after a while, place the bowl back on top of the saucepan on low heat and add a little coconut oil to bring it back to a drizzly consistently.

nice cream sandwiches

makes 12 slices
prep time: 35 minutes
chill time: 6 hours

An ice cream sandwich is probably the most enjoyable and convenient way to have ice cream. This is made with two gooey layers of raw fudge brownie filled with a layer of nice cream made from *oats*. I know.

brownie
1¼ cups raw almonds
¾ cup dates, pitted
6 tbsp cocoa powder
3 tbsp tapioca flour
1 tsp vanilla extract
pinch of salt

nice cream
1 cup rolled oats
2 cups boiling water
½ cup coconut cream
(page 31)
¼ cup maple syrup
1½ tsp vanilla extract

Add the oats to a small saucepan with the boiling water and cook for 15-20 minutes until the oats are very thick and have absorbed all the moisture from the water. Set aside to cool.

For the brownie, add the almonds to a food processor and blend until grainy. Use a spoon to scrape any of the ground almonds stuck to the edges or at the base of the food processor. Add the dates, cocoa powder, tapioca flour, vanilla extract, salt and blend until a dough is formed.

Put the dough on parchment paper and roll it out roughly into a 12 x 7-inch rectangle. Place in a baking pan and freeze while you make the nice cream.

Go back to the oats and stir in the coconut oil until it's melted.

Clean and dry the food processor. Add the cooked oats, coconut cream, maple syrup and vanilla extract and blend until smooth.

Take the brownie dough out of the freezer and slice it in half. Place half of the brownie down, hitch up the sides of the parchment paper and pour in the nice cream. Use a spatula to smooth over and put in the freezer to set for an hour. Place the other half of the brownie on top of the nice cream filling and leave it to set in the freezer for another 5 hours. With a large, sharp knife, slice into 12 bars. Allow to rest at room temperature for 5 minutes before serving.

Store in an airtight container in the freezer for up to 3 months.

notes
If your dates aren't soft, soak them in a bowl of hot water for at least an hour.

lina jabbari

A recipe developer, food stylist and designer based in Sussex, UK. Founder of @thathealthjunkie where she found a passion of sharing her recipe creations with her extended online community.

Sweet by Lina Jabbari

@thathealthjunkie

www.thathealthjunkie.com

This book contains information that is intended to help the readers be better informed consumers of health care. It is presented as general advice on health care. Always consult your doctor for your individual needs.

The information provided within this book is for general informational purposes only. While we try to keep the information up-to-date and correct, there are no representations or warranties, express or implied, about the completeness, accuracy, reliability, suitability or availability with respect to the information, products, services, or related graphics contained in this book for any purpose. Any use of this information is at your own risk.

acknowledgements

Big thanks to my family for tip-toeing around me in the kitchen while I was full on Godzilla. Thank you for tolerating my heavy, heavy mood swings for all those failed bakes.

Grandma - Thank you for teaching me to be kind and patient with myself. I'm grateful to be graced by your energy and pure light. Watching you bring people together through the food you lovingly make, is what inspires me to do what I do.

Mum - Your honesty wasn't what I wanted to hear at times but I needed it to make me do better. I wouldn't have pushed myself as hard as I did, nor would I be where I am today without you. And although you don't consider yourself a baker, I was always impressed by how you managed to bake a quick cake when we craved one.

Maryam - What would I do without your expertise? I'm so lucky to be so close to a dessert critic with impeccible taste. If I knew you liked it, I knew I did good.

Farina - Your genuine enthusiasm and love for my bakes gave me the assurance and confidence I sometimes needed to know that my bakes had to be shared with the world.

Farhad - I can't even put into words how grateful I am for you giving me the space I needed to make it possible for me to work on this project.

Emily - My bestie, you've been by my side since day one and I am so grateful for you. You always keep it real and I can always trust your input. Thank you for letting me constantly harass you for your design expertise.

Noor - My no1 hype woman, my sister, my babe. Your words of wisdom got me through the down times when I was filled with doubt. Your consistent support throughout the years means everything to me and I'm so blessed to have you.

Fateme Zan Dayee - Your words of consistent encouragement and pep talks, gave me the nudge I needed to get started with this book.

Bahare - Thank you for exposing me to all the food/ desserts that I didn't even know existed, we had the best times and it gave me great inspo.

Nina - Thank you for believing in me and making me believe in myself. I'll never forget what you did for me and I can't wait for the day I can do the same for you.

Tracy and Maja - The talented bakers that got me involved in baking from a young age which further sparked my love and curiosity for baking.

My editor Rochelle - For helping me organise the chaos. Thank you for your patience, understanding and hard work.

Dmitri - My word ninja. Thanks for helping me sound smart and bugging me to finish it.

Thank you to all the people that taste-tested my recipes.

Thank you to my proofreaders - Emily, Leoni, Ellie and Heidi.

All the chefs, cooks and the people online that inspired me to start my own journey.

Thank you to my beaut community at that health junkie, this wouldn't have happened without you. Your support means everything and I love you all!

My readers - Thank you for your support, I hope these recipes bring as much joy to you as they do for me.

index